MHCC WITHDRAWN

GV 425 .D475 2006

Design for fun

D1774185

Design for Fun

PART I:
designing a playground

PART II:
playspaces

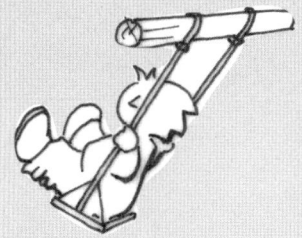

Edition 2006

Project concept: Carles Broto
Editorial coordinator: Jacobo Krauel
Texts for the projects were contributed by the designers
translated by Amber Ockrassa
Graphic design and production: Dimitris Kottas
Part 1, designing a playground: Marta Rojals

Cover photograph © Doug Snower Photography

© Carles Broto i Comerma
Jonqueres, 10, 1-5
08003 Barcelona, Spain
Tel.: +34 93 301 21 99
Fax: +34-93-301 00 21
E-mail: info@linksbooks.net
www. linksbooks.net

No part of this publication may be reproduced, stored in retrieval system or transmitted in any form or means, electronic, mechanical, photocopying, recording or otherwise, without the prior written permission of the owner of the Copyright.

designing a playground

Index

Designing a Playground   5

Growing
What are we going to play?

1. The Play Area   8

1.1 Interacting with the Surroundings
The lay of the land
Plants
Water
1.2 Differentiated Spaces and Uses
Inside and out
Everything in its place
1.3 Let's All go to the Park
No barriers
Accesses and routes
Side protection for paths
1.4 Up and Down
Steps and stairs
Ladders
Ramps
1.5 Paving
1.6 Take a Deep Breath

2. Playground Equipment   16

2.1 Things to Keep in Mind...
Materials
Handrails and railings
Boundaries
Supports
Joints, bolts, edges
2.2 Slipping and Sliding
Types of slide
Parts of the slide
Widths and surfaces
2.3 Swinging and Rocking
Types of swing sets
Parts of the swing
Distances and surfaces
2.4 Climbing
Climbing on rigid equipment
Climbing on flexible equipment
2.5 Composite Playground Equipment
2.6 Playing with Nothing - Shapes
2.7 Learning through the Senses
Sounds
Watch, see, observe
Touch and texture
...and smell!
2.8 Building - Playing with Sand and Mud
2.9 Splashing Around - Playing with Water
2.10 On Wheels

3. Ensuring Safe Play Conditions   28

3.1 Padding Impact
3.2 Minimum Space
The area of impact
Obstacle-free fall height
3.3 Protection Against Getting Stuck
Getting the head or neck stuck
Getting the extremities stuck

Designing a Playground

We have now seen how each designer's creativity and imagination are manifested in a thousand different ways and with exceptional results. Some of the play spaces and their components may seem elaborate, others less so. Even behind the seemingly simple designs lies a sense of experimentation and the will to provide good, fitting stimuli for children. Furthermore, the design of a recreational space must answer to this need, while taking into account a series of aspects that go beyond mere formal discourse.
This appendix deals with these topics in a structured and straightforward manner. There are three sections, which are preceded by an introduction reflecting on the activity of playing and on the different ways that children play. The first two sections comprise, respectively, a number of guidelines and suggestions for planning a playground, and the design of playground equipment. The third is a concise section dealing with safety issues from a design perspective.
In sum, this appendix complements the practical examples that we have already seen, providing a series of basic norms for drawing up the first sketches of a new playground or playground equipment and helping define the guidelines toward a definitive layout.

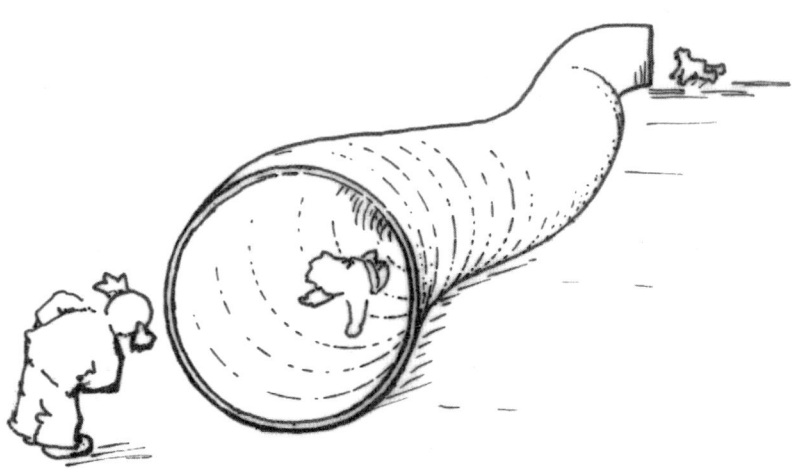

Growing

Children go through different stages marked by evolving ways of playing as they grow. While we need to understand these stages in order to create suitable play spaces for each age group, it is also important to remember that all children are different and that preferences and needs may vary among, and even within, each age group.

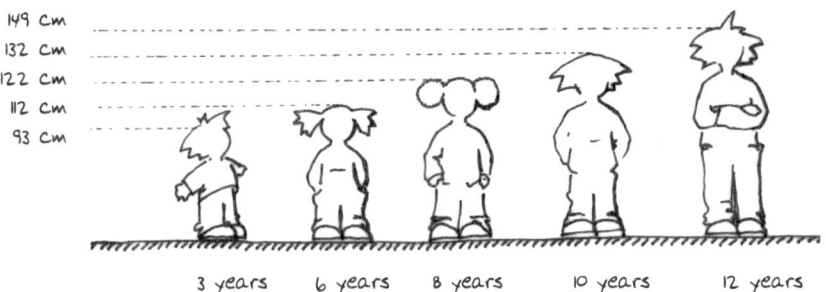

As we grow, the games that we enjoy also evolve.

Broadly speaking, we can establish the following growth stages, and the play habits observed in each phase:

0-3 years

Children acquire their formative experiences and learn to control their own movement in the first three years of their lives. They usually play alone and tend toward experimentation with touch, sight and sound. Playing in sand, clay, water, swings and slides (the last two with the help of an adult) are appropriate for this stage.

3-6 years

Between 3 and 6 years of age, and with the onset of social awareness, children usually play in groups, thereby fostering interpersonal relationships and sociability. Children in this age group enjoy activities which represent something else; for example, they play with abstract elements, tables, benches, as well as with swings, slides and movable equipment.

6-8 years

From age 6 to 8 children gravitate toward activities which involve movement and action; activities which develop both organizational and physical skills. Children in this age group enjoy testing their dexterity with elements such as climbing nets and other more or less complex structures that call upon different motor responses.

8-10 years, and upward

As adolescence nears, children opt for grouping together, but without adult supervision or interference from younger children. Structured games with objective rules played in groups or teams tend to predominate at this age. They also like to demonstrate their powers of balance and coordination in more complex climbing equipment.

What are we going to play?

Keeping active. Physical games.

Highly physical play activities, such as jumping, running, cycling, crawling, climbing or sliding often require nothing more than a good space equipped with adequate protection against bumps and falls. Nonetheless, it is always advisable to ensure some form of modular play equipment, structures and varied terrain, all of which provides a range of possibilities for interaction and dynamic games.

The traditional game of "tag", a type of physical game.

Getting along. Social games.

Social or relational games are those that involve chasing, hiding and role-playing in groups; imagination is the primary tool used in such activities. Since only very basic means are required to stimulate the imagination, it is more effective to provide abstract, suggestive elements which the children will adapt in their own way.

Hide-and-seek: social games do not require complicated elements.

Imagining. Creative games.

Material which can be molded or transformed such as sand, grass, water, gravel or clay is used in this type of play. It's hard for a child to keep still when presented with these materials; the physical properties of such elements enable children to develop a wide variety of activities in which the imagination and creativity are of prime importance - qualities of which the smallest children are true masters!

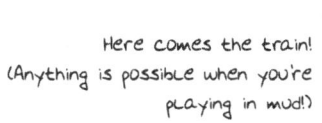 

Here comes the train! (Anything is possible when you're playing in mud!)

Experimenting. Sensorial games.

Although the senses are involved in all human activity, children are the true pioneers in experimenting with them, which is why those play elements that necessarily involve sensorial experience are especially recommendable. In addition to elements designed for stimulating the sense of touch, auditory, visual and even olfactory stimuli can be incorporated.

 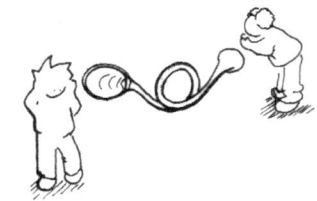

Channeled sound.

...and playing in peace and quiet

Playing peacefully in the sand.

Providing opportunities for rest and reflection in a playground is just as important as encouraging physical activity. A child's choice to play alone, quietly, should therefore be respected. In order to create the appropriate environment for achieving this, one or various spaces should be set aside and shielded from the noise and activity of the other play areas. In so doing, we provide a setting where children can concentrate on their activity free from outside interference or distractions. At the same time, we gain a peaceful spot that adults can also enjoy. Here, we can set up sand boxes, tables and benches and also ensure that the area is adequately protected from excessive exposure to the sun.

1. The Play Area

Before beginning the design of a play area, it's a good idea to pay a visit to a playground that is already in use. There, we can observe the children's reactions to certain spaces and play equipment and take note of how each situation unfolds. Children can be the harshest of judges in their own way, which is why a positive response to a certain playground arrangement or element is a highly gratifying experience for the designer of that space.
For example, kids enjoy variety in their playground equipment and spaces; that is, the opportunity to play any number of games or activities. When something doesn't bring about the desired result, they get bored and quickly throw themselves into something else. To avoid boredom, the play equipment should be attractive and suitable for each age group and for different levels of activity. It should also provide diverse stimuli for promoting a child's development - equipment designed to encourage social skills, integration with others and respect for the environment. It doesn't take much to achieve this; no matter how limited the available ground space may be nor how restricted the budget, it is important to never underestimate the possibilities of a future playground. Excellent play opportunities can be provided with even the minimum of effort and resources.
The freedom to design, however, must be subject to regulations for making sure the equipment is safe for its users. Everything in a children's park or playground must comply with each region's specific technical norms concerning playground equipment. The safety precepts and dimensional requisites on the following pages, unless otherwise stated, correspond to the European standards on playground equipment (1176:1998), published by the European Committee for Standardization.
The following information should not be taken as a substitution for local norms. It is herein included in order to provide some useful guidelines for the professional designer as well as the layperson. These basic recommendations will be of use in drawing up an outline for the future playground, play equipment or even a private backyard, safe in the knowledge that the spaces for our children are being looked after in a creative and responsible way.

1.1 Interacting with the Surroundings

The lay of the land

The first conditioning factor in any future playground is the configuration of the ground surface where it is going to be placed. If the occasion (and privilege) of being able to work on natural terrain arises, we can greatly enhance and simplify the design of the playground if we respect the existing topography.
Since children respond more enthusiastically to irregular forms than to uniform, rectilinear shapes, the possibilities of a natural area in and of itself for providing ample play opportunities are considerable indeed.

Playing with the rise and fall of the land.

We can, for example, experiment with the anomalies of the terrain, making use of changes in level, accentuating or softening slopes and setting up different zones at different heights. Children enjoy imagining adventures, "getting lost" and finding their bearings, rolling down the slopes, playing hide-and-seek with the rise and fall of the land or "king of the mountain".
In any event, even if the site offers few opportunities from the start, we can always add the design of hills, slopes, caves and a variety of other elements that provide good stimuli for playing, while also encouraging children to explore the environment and hone their spatial abilities. With such simple touches as these, the results couldn't be better!

Lengthened, curvilinear forms are preferable over squares and lines.

Vegetation

Vegetation is a highly valuable element in the design of any space intended for use by children, whether for its environmental or aesthetic aspects, or simply for fun.

Plants improve air quality and serve as a protective barrier against rain and sun, both on their own or in conjunction with pergolas or similar structures. Additionally, dense plant species mitigate wind and reduce noise - or at least alter sounds by generating their own. And, of course, plants are a natural habitat for birds and other small animals, making it a prime consideration to conserve and protect any existing vegetated area there may be on the site.

In any event, bringing in new plant and tree species can contribute to the creation of a unique environment that will enhance the educational properties of the activities to take place in the park. For example, if we plant deciduous plant species, sunlight will penetrate the canopy in the wintertime, while plenty of shade will be ensured for the summer months. Also, with fruit trees, children receive firsthand knowledge of seasonal life cycles.

It is especially important to conserve and incorporate any existing trees into the project, unless they present a danger to the health of the children. Mature tees offer an appealing, solid aspect which saplings and recently-planted trees have not yet acquired. Furthermore, their placement might lay the groundwork for the layout of a design that will undoubtedly reflect sensitivity and respect for the environment, invaluable qualities in any project these days.

Tall plants and trees mitigate the effects of the sun and rain.

We should respect existing tree species, working them into the design if possible...

...and protect the youngest ones.

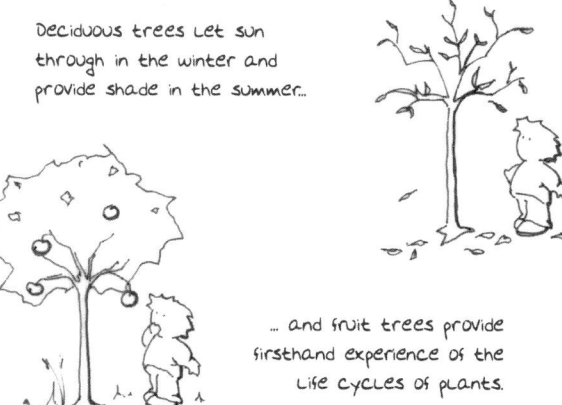

Deciduous trees let sun through in the winter and provide shade in the summer...

...and fruit trees provide firsthand experience of the life cycles of plants.

Playground activities can be very harmful to the vegetation, especially to shrubs and other low-lying plant species. Thus, wherever new plants are added, resistant species appropriate to the environment with a high capacity for regeneration should be chosen.

Before deciding upon a given species, it is important to know if the park is going to receive sufficient care at regular intervals. Untended vegetation may mar the overall look of any playground as well as involve risks for the children. This does not mean that, faced with the prospect of scarce upkeep, we should have to do without plants. On the contrary, there are numerous species that do not require special attention and that produce excellent results.

Water

Children particularly enjoy water, even more so when they are allowed to touch it or play in it, as we will see in section 3.9.
Any existing natural water should be conserved and worked into the project as far as possible. Highly valuable ecosystems depend on creeks, canals, ponds, swamps and natural springs; the project should work around and respect them. These water habitats will also encourage children to observe and learn about life cycles and the natural environment.

Aquatic ecosystems are a valuable source of learning about the natural environment.

1.2 Differentiated Spaces and Uses

The park should be well separated from potentially unsafe areas and have clearly marked accesses.

Inside and out

For obvious safety reasons, the borders of a playground should be well defined. Areas where safety conditions cannot be controlled, such as surrounding roads, must be physically separated. These delimitations can be achieved with natural elements, such as shrubs, for example, or using artificial solutions, such as walls and fences.
Bearing in mind how children love to scamper up and over objects in a playground, care should be taken to avoid making these peripheral structures look climbable. Their height and surface treatment should be such that kids are not tempted to climb, sit or stand on them. Additionally, it is important to clearly identify the park's entrances and exits and to make them easy to access from primary roads and circulation routes.

Everything in its place

Ensuring a certain degree of organization in a playground is a necessary aspect so that children learn to find themselves within a space and get their bearings among different play areas.
A prior classification of the activities that are to take place in the playground is a good place to start; it will help establish spatial relationships according to criteria of function and use. For example, we will differentiate the zones intended for group activities and those where children can play individually: noisy, physical activities should be kept apart from the area set aside for quieter games. This area, in turn, could be placed in relation to the areas of the park set aside for rest and contemplation or at the outer limits of the site.

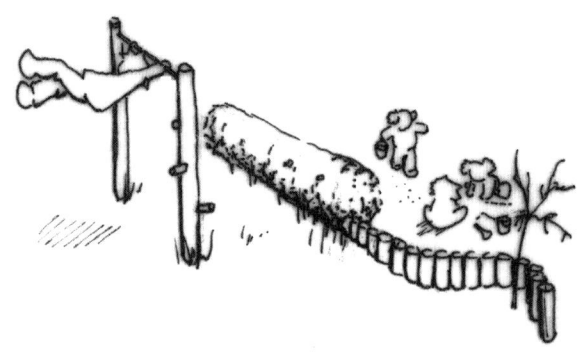

Very different or incompatible activities should be appropriately separated.

The playground should be sheltered from the wind.

Borders between different or incompatible play areas should also be easily recognizable, whether they be physical, visual or acoustic markers. Although these areas should be differentiated and independent, they should nonetheless be somehow linked so as to encourage relations between different groups.

A few more details to keep in mind: whatever layout chosen in the end, we should consider whether the play areas, especially those for the smallest children, can be easily seen from other points of the park. It is also recommendable to set up sunny and shady areas, places sheltered from the wind and rain, all according to the climate and necessities of each geographic zone.

1.3 Let's All Go to the Park

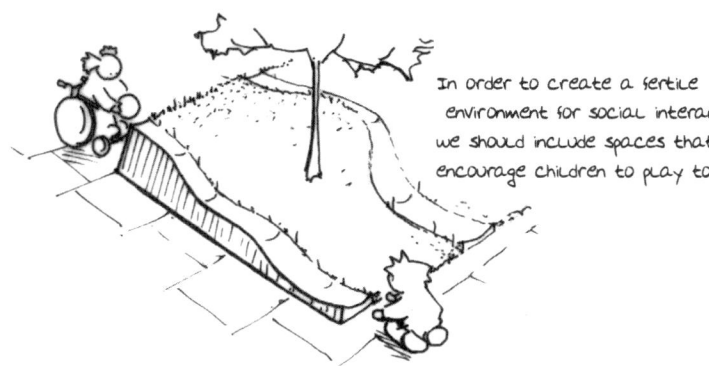

In order to create a fertile environment for social interaction, we should include spaces that encourage children to play together.

Above all, a good design must be based on the idea that all children are different and therefore may have very different needs. All children should find equal opportunities for entertainment and recreation in a playground; to meet this goal, we should come up with play spaces that allow them to interact and learn together.

We should pay special attention to the smallest children and those with mental or physical limitations, these being groups for whom play time is especially important.

No barriers

Up until only a few years ago, playground design, as with many urban projects, did not take into account the fact that many visitors may have difficulties in freely moving about the established spaces. Fortunately, public spaces are now designed to be accessible to the handicapped; each geographic zone has its own accessibility regulations to meet this end.

Ensuring a barrier-free space involves more than simply leaving out equipment or objects that may obstruct the use of a space; it also means that we should consider incorporating specific elements - without making excessive alterations or compromising the design - that can be enjoyed by all visitors.

The smallest children and those with some sort of handicap need special attention.

keeping everyone in mind: for example, a raised planter helps protect plants while also allowing all users to reach it.

Accesses and routes

Paying particular attention to accesses and routes in a playground is fundamental for ensuring equality of conditions for all children. For example, if stairs and slopes are complemented with ramps, we resolve one of the most frequent problems of accessibility for persons with reduced mobility. If it is not possible to make the route flat, slopes should be moderated to less than 5% and include corresponding resting spots at regular intervals, given that moving along inclined surfaces is especially tiring for users with motor difficulties.

Alternatives to steps (a ramp, for example) should be included on all playground equipment.

It is advisable to route various types of paths through the playground, each one diverging from the main path so that children can freely explore. These itineraries can overlap, split apart and provide alternative routes while at the same time enriching the design of the park. Narrow paths and cul-de-sacs should be avoided in all cases, as they are trouble spots where children might collide. We can also set up circuits for tricycles and bikes that are sufficiently differentiated from the footpaths in order to avoid possible collisions.

Different routes or itineraries to discover.

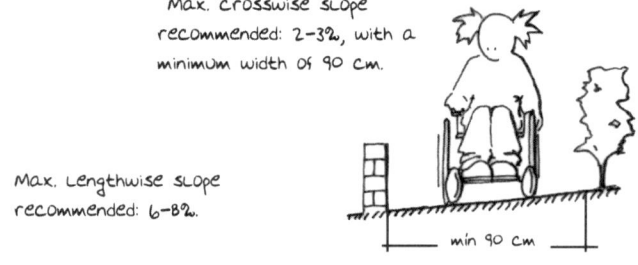

Max. crosswise slope recommended: 2-3%, with a minimum width of 90 cm.

Max. lengthwise slope recommended: 6-8%.

Following accessibility criteria, a route, installation or space might be:
- Adapted, if it meets all of the necessary functional and dimensional conditions to be used comfortably by persons with impaired mobility or sensory abilities.
- Practicable, if it meets the minimum conditions to be used by persons with reduced mobility or sensory abilities.
- Convertible, when it can become practicable or adapted through simple, low-cost modifications.

Itineraries	Adapted	Practicable	Convertible
Width	90-180 cm	90-120 cm	90 cm
Maximum lenthwise slope (for ramps)	6-8%	8-10%	10-12%
Maximum crosswise slope	2%	3%	5%

Side protection for paths

Steep slopes or inclines where falls are more likely should be protected by handrails or curbs. Sidewalks, for example, should be included in tight spots or in areas where it may be hard to get through; and an identifiable change in material should mark practicable itineraries for people with poor eyesight.
The need for fixtures such as paved sidewalks, curbs and handrails is dictated by the degree of accessibility at any given point and by the particularities of the site and of contiguous vertical levels, in which case it is also necessary to check local accessibility regulations. Most regulations also state that branches, leaning tree trunks and other vertical elements might be dangerous if they overhang or otherwise interfere with footpaths; therefore, none of these elements should be within the range of the footpath at a height below 2.10 meters.

Handrails should be included wherever there are obstacles.

Paths should be marked and should include handrails where there are pronounced changes in level.

1.4 Up and Down

Steps and stairs

Contrary to appearances, stairs are often more comfortable than ramps for people with impaired mobility. We should therefore pay special attention to this aspect of the design, adhering to regulations regarding accessibility in public spaces.

Adapted stairs should have handrails on both sides.

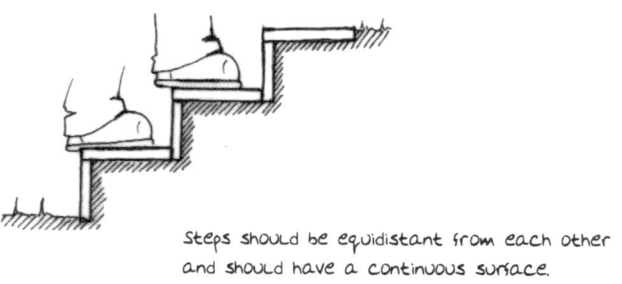

Steps should be equidistant from each other and should have a continuous surface.

Steps and stairs on play equipment are different from conventional steps and stairs in that they must comply with a unique set of requisites dictating size and safety. Summing up the characteristics common to both types of access, stairs should have a constant inclination with equidistant steps and should be of uniform construction. Especially long stairs should be divided, with platforms placed at intermediate intervals.
The upper surface should be covered with some sort of non-slip material to avoid slips and falls. Additionally, handrails should be placed on both sides of adapted stairs in order to ensure that all users can get a good grasp on it.

Ladders

Ladders are used primarily for enabling access to the uppermost point of a structure or playground equipment. The most common ladders are generally those providing access to slides and modular equipment with platforms at varying heights. Being inclined, ladders occupy very little surface area, a characteristic which makes them appropriate for most playground equipment, which is usually on a smaller scale to accommodate the youngest children.

The crossbars and steps of a ladder should be placed at equidistant intervals.

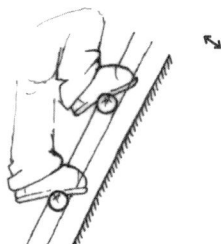

The space above each crossbar should allow for sufficient foot support.

As opposed to standard ladders, their use requires foot and hand support, although a handrail will do if necessary. Crossbars and steps should therefore have adequate, unobstructed space for foot- and hand-holds and should be equidistant and stationary. Wherever possible, playground equipment should include alternative access routes (as opposed to conventional ladders) so that children with motor impairments can use it without difficulty.

Ramps

Getting around on sloped surfaces can be especially tiring for users with impaired mobility: a ramp which is too long or with an inadequate slope can render a path useless for those who really need it. Therefore, we should pay special attention to the length and maximum degree of inclination of the ramps to make them comfortable to use and effective.

Bearing in mind the physical effort involved in getting around for people with motor impairments, it is important to keep the minimum distance between the ladder and its ramp alternative.

The ramp should have a non-slip surface.

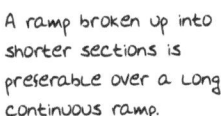

A ramp broken up into shorter sections is preferable over a long, continuous ramp.

We should also remember that not just any sloped surface will function as a ramp. Technically, a ramp is a surface with a slope of between 5% and 10%, and up to 12% in extreme cases. The degree of the slope should be constant along the entire length and, in the event that the ramp has to be especially long, it should be broken up into shorter sections which are separated by level platforms at each turn. The handrails or walls should begin at the lowermost point and the surface should be non-slip.

The specific details for the correct dimensions of the ramps are also included in the regulations governing such structures in each geographic zone.

1.5 Paving

Depending on the necessities and characteristics of the location, various types of surface treatments are used in playgrounds. Thus, a footpath requires a paving material different from that used in the swings and slide area, where there is a consistently higher risk of falls. (Section 4.1 contains information on material for padding falls.)

In general, all paving in a playground should be stable, firm, able to pad falls, with a texture that is not too rough and a non-slip surface in both wet and dry conditions. Naturally, any joints or discontinuities in the paving should be treated so as to not obstruct movement in a wheelchair or on crutches.

Different combinations of textures and colors in paving in order to achieve a specific effect -whether for informative or purely aesthetic reasons- can be highly inspiring for kids. This can be done where we wish to provide information, mark a change in direction or a transition from one play area to another, to distinguish areas for rest and relaxation, and so forth. Additionally, changes in texture can be detected by blind children and even particularly bright colors can be perceived by visually impaired persons.

Paving should be stable and have a non-slip surface.

1.6 Take a Deep Breath

Areas for resting

A space, no matter how small, where a child can sit quietly and relax or gather strength to continue playing is an invaluable addition to any playground.

In larger playgrounds, it is a good idea to create rest zones at regular intervals. Such zones must comply with the corresponding accessibility criteria. European standards recommend that in adapted itineraries the distance between these zones should range between 45 and 60 meters; and in practicable itineraries, this distance should not exceed 200 meters.

A rest zone might be composed simply of a set of benches or other seating elements that are protected from the wind and rain. An open area equivalent to a circle of one and half meters in diameter should be set alongside the benches in order to allow wheelchair users to maneuver without difficulty.

Finally, the rest zone should not be set in some leftover, fringe area, since another essential function of such a zone is to encourage children to socialize with others. They should therefore be located near play areas that display different characteristics and that are intended for different age groups.

Space for wheelchairs set alongside the benches.

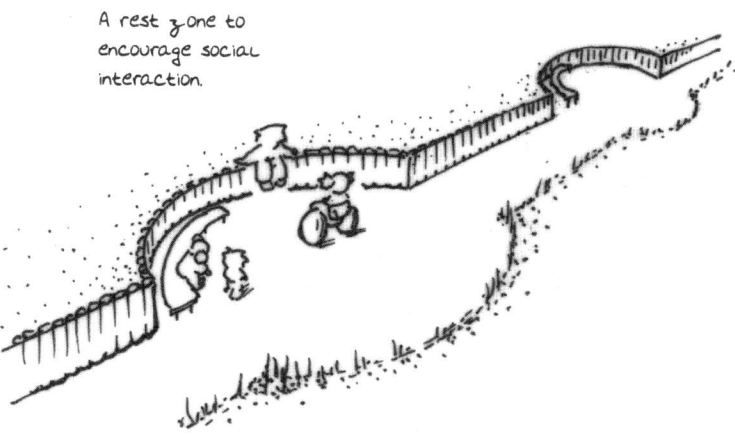

A rest zone to encourage social interaction.

2. Playground Equipment

Although there is a seeming infinity of standardized playground equipment on the market, designers often prefer to create their own pieces, custom-tailoring them to a specific playground and its peculiarities. These one-off pieces come to define the playground's distinct character. Most of the projects featured in this book use exclusive playground equipment in their design - equipment which may or may not be combined with more conventional structures.

Building play equipment does not just involve coming up with an attractive and fun design, but rather calls for ensuring that the finished product is completely safe for children. The choice of basic material as well as surface finishes and the addition of elements to safeguard against falls are all equally as important, making it often more comfortable and preferable to rely on professionals specializing in the field of playground design.

Numerous companies and playground equipment manufacturers specializing in highly creative and innovative playground equipment have sprung up in recent years. These new designs show a clear tendency toward interactivity in an effort to integrate educational functions with the playground's more obvious reason for being: fun. Thus, sound-producing elements or games with water, for example, are now frequently worked into the design of play areas.

Classic playground equipment, such as slides and swings, are still widely used; in fact, they have never gone out of style and are included alongside custom-designed pieces in most newly constructed playgrounds. While swings have undergone scarce formal variations, a certain evolution can be seen in the design of slides, in material as well as shape, the overall end-goal being to make them both more innovative and safer.

However, in contrast to the newer and more or less sophisticated equipment, there are always those tried and true elements which do not depend on the availability of a large budget: the classic sand box is a good example, or simple wide open spaces for running and playing. After all, it's the imagination that counts.

2.1 Things to Keep in Mind...

Materials

Materials which facilitate durability, hygiene and ease of maintenance should be opted for when constructing playground equipment.

To begin with, neither potentially toxic elements nor raw metals (which rust or may act as conduits for electricity) should be used. Metal should be painted, galvanized or otherwise treated to prevent rust. Wood is a good alternative to metal - it should be of a kind that does not splinter and, in any event, should be thoroughly treated (meaning more than a simple surface work-over) to avoid splinters or irregularities that can snag or cut. If synthetic materials are chosen, they must also be durable enough to avoid splintering and cracking.

The treatment of surface finishes, especially on rough or uneven material, is another basic consideration in greatly reducing the risk of injury. (See section 4.3).

wood should not crack or splinter.

Handrails and railings

Handrails and railings are the most common safety elements in playground equipment. Handrails and railings serve not only as protection against falls, but they can also be gripped and used as support and stability. They should therefore be designed for an easy grip, according to the size requirements of the corresponding regulation.

Railings protect against falls.

Handrails should be easy to get a hold on.

The height and diameter of such lateral protection are established according to their placement - whether on ladders, ramps, walkways or raised platforms - and must comply with accessibility requirements for the area or equipment. The European standard stipulates that handrails and railings be placed at a height between 60 and 85 centimeters from the platform, ladder or ramp; recommended width and diameter of handrails is between 25 and 32 millimeters.

Boundaries

Whether or not boundaries are needed depends on the age group which will be using the equipment and also on the height of support surface to which the children will climb.
As with railings, boundaries also prevent falls from raised platforms, while also keeping children from climbing to certain heights. The design of the boundary, therefore, should be such that it does not encourage climbing, standing or sitting on it.

Barriers also keep children from reaching certain heights.

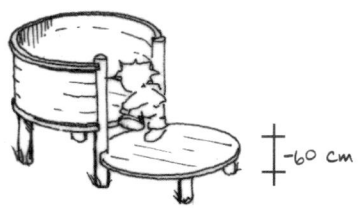

Barriers starting at 60 centimeters in height above the play surface are appropriate for play equipment for toddlers.

The boundary should completely enclose the perimeter of the raised surface, with the logical exception of the portion intended for entering and exiting the platform. If there are openings, they should be smaller than the size of a small child in order to prevent them from slipping through or getting stuck in the gaps. Boundaries should have a minimum height of 70 cm. from the surface of the platform, ladder or ramp.

Supports

Many play elements feature supports - which work indiscriminately for both hands and feet - for gripping, stabilizing or climbing. An effective handgrip should be of a size and placement so as to allow children to get their hand completely around it. It should be securely affixed to the main structure so that it will not come off or turn. According to the EU standard for an effective handgrip, it should be no wider than 60 millimeters, with a cross section of between 16 and 45 millimeters in order to be securely gripped. (It is recommended that those measuring 16 millimeters not be of wood, as such a thin piece may break.)

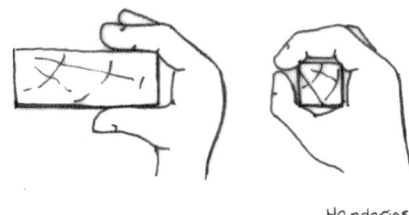

Handgrips

Joints, bolts, edges

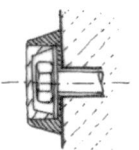 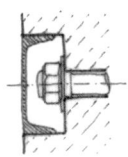

Potentially dangerous protrusions should be protected.

This category encompasses the outer edges of a piece of play equipment, as well as the system for affixing each of its components. As a safety precaution, sharp edges, pointy shapes and dangerous angles should all be avoided. Welded pieces should have smooth surfaces, and anything that anchors or holds the structure in place should be solid and stable. Nails should lie flush with the main structure, bolts should be covered by plastic caps and screws should not protrude more than 8 mm.

2.2 Slipping and Sliding

Kids have always been drawn to any type of inclined surface down which they can slip and slide, which is why slides are such a popular feature in a playground. It is rare indeed the playground that doesn't have a slide. Although there are an endless number of models on the market, it is often more appropriate to custom design a slide for a specific playground, whether the particularities of the site call for it, or whether it fits in with the general theme of the project or simply because we have the means to do so. No matter how valid a particular design may appear to be, bear in mind that it may not be apt for children; there are certain considerations of safety and size, according to the corresponding regulations, that must be adhered to. Here are some helpful general considerations:

Types of slide

Few pieces of playground equipment are available in such a variety of shapes and models as the slide. Their very nature is open to an endless number of options, from the standard freestanding slide with a ladder to the most complex models, which feature curves (even helicoids) and waves.

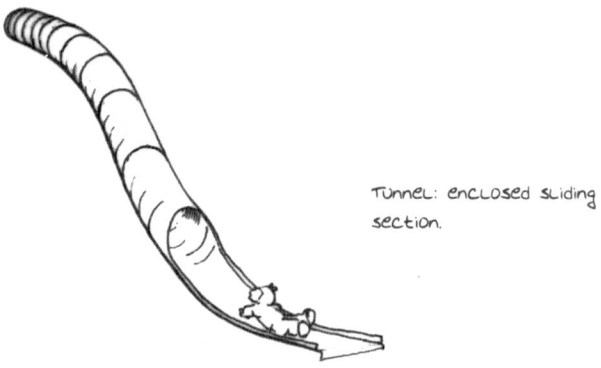

Tunnel: enclosed sliding section.

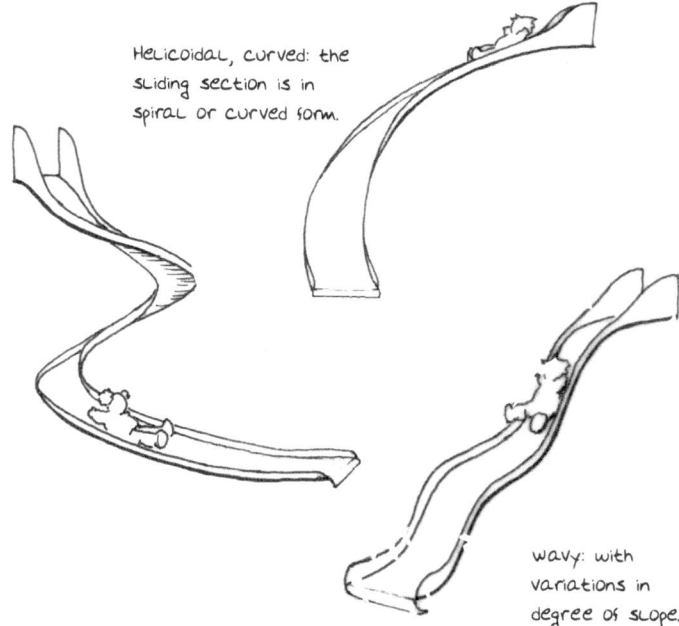

Helicoidal, curved: the sliding section is in spiral or curved form.

wavy: with variations in degree of slope.

Parts of the slide

No aspect of the shape of a slide is merely coincidental, but rather responds to series of requisites that make it safe and effective; not just any sloped surface can be considered a slide. Basically, this apparatus is made up of three parts: the starting point, the main section (the "slide" itself) and the finishing point. Each of these components slopes to a differing degree.
The starting point should be the same width as the main section and the transition from one section to the next should be smooth and continuous. It should be long enough to allow a child to comfortably and easily reach it and sit down.

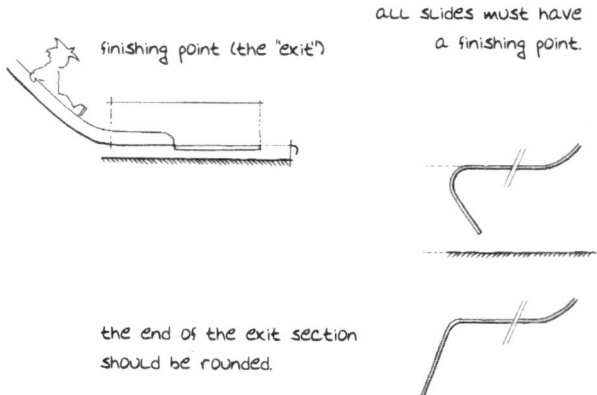

finishing point (the "exit")

all slides must have a finishing point.

the end of the exit section should be rounded.

While most are open, it is becoming more common to find slides that are partially or entirely enclosed: tunnel slides.

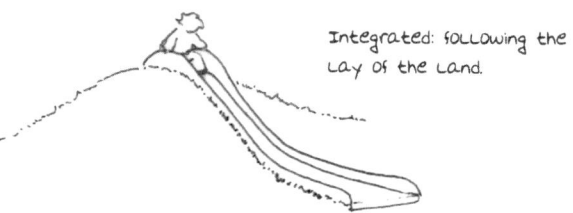

Integrated: following the lay of the land.

Terrain permitting, a good option is to integrate the slide into the lay of the land, thus achieving a more accessible solution for children with motor difficulties. This type of slide is one of the most visually attractive, each one becoming a unique piece in its own right.

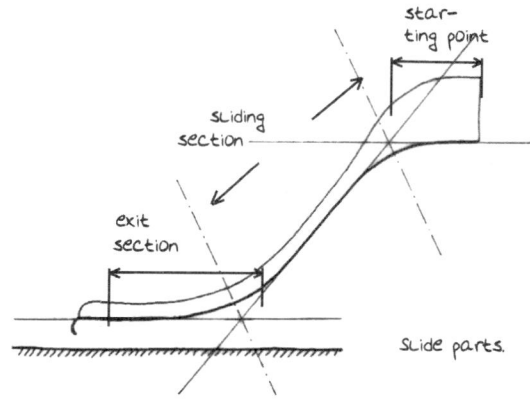

slide parts.

All slides must feature an "exit" (the finishing point) in order to help the child maintain balance, decrease the possibility of possible crashes and make it easier for the child to get off the equipment. All finishes should be rounded or curved in order to avoid cuts and other minor injuries. The tunnel section of covered slides should be continuous until the final "sliding" portion, without including the exit point, which should be open as well.
Side protection is another highly important feature of the slide. It fulfills the dual function of ensuring that the child does not fall off and providing hand support. This feature can be perpendicular, curved or angled; the corners should be continuous and rounded in order to avoid cuts and other accidents.

Widths and surfaces

The standard straight, open slide with a sliding section longer than one and a half meters should have a width measuring either less than 70 centimeters, or more than 95 centimeters. These dimensions ensure than children do not get stuck on the way down or tumble over on their sides, possibly getting hurt.

In curved or spiral slides, the width of the sliding section should be less than 70 centimeters. The minimum width and height of the interior of a tunnel slide should be 75 centimeters (the height being measured perpendicularly from the surface of the sliding section.

As all of the elements of a slide should avoid discontinuities that might snag clothing or where fingers can get stuck, it is highly recommended that the surface of the sliding section be of one piece. Metal slides should be installed in the shade so as to avoid possible burns caused by excessive sunlight heating the surface.

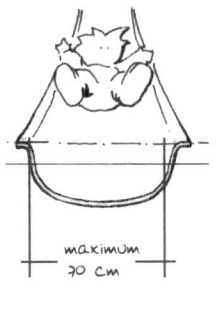
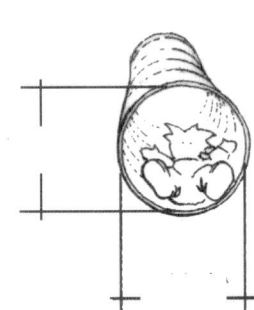

In tunnel slides...

...in open slides.

2.3 Swinging and Rocking

Swing sets, as with the slide, have become classics in playground equipment. The rocking of a swing has a calming effect, most notably with small children; it also helps develop the faculties of balance and coordination. Again, as with the slide, if we choose to custom design a swing set for a specific playground we must follow the technical specifications guiding the construction of playground equipment. Following are a few general design considerations.

Types of swing sets

A general primary classification of swing types is how many points of suspension they feature, one or various.

Swings with more that one suspension point are those with one or more axes of rotation. A swing with one axis of rotation produces a rocking motion perpendicular to the load bearing bar. Those with various axes of rotation enable a rocking motion perpendicular or parallel to the bar; in this case, the seat may hang from one or more bars.

As a safety measure, it is not advisable to include this type of swing in conjunction with other equipment in a set.

Among the swings with a single point of suspension are the well-known classics using a tire; although there are now safer alterna-

Swing with two points of suspension and a single axis of rotation.

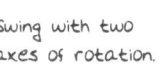

Swing with two axes of rotation.

that are designed to look like tires and come in varying sizes. this type of swing oscillates in all directions, special care ⌐d be taken to ensure safe distances from nearby structures ⌐ith the supporting structure of the swing itself. It is crucial to ⌐sure the suspension is firmly anchored. The fact that various ⌐will all be swinging at the same time and that the rotation point ⌐eed to vary erratically should come to bear on calculating the ⌐struction.

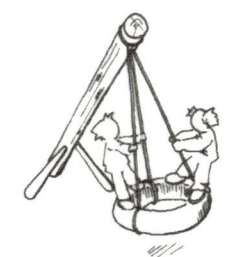

Swings with a single point of suspension allow for multiple uses.

P⌐ s of the swing

A seat and the elements from which it hangs, in turn fastened to one or more load bearing bars and a structure anchored to the ground are the basic components of a swing.

The seat should be designed to hold just one user at a time. There are two broad groups of seat: flat, with neither back support nor side guards, and the so-called "harness" type, which provides greater support for the smallest users or those with motor impairments. Materials with even a minimum degree of pliability should be chosen for the seats. Metal and wood are not recommended, as they could cause serious injury in the event of a child being bumped or hit by the seat.

Swings with one point of suspension can have platforms or tires intended to be used while standing. The material from which the seat hangs should not, in any event, be completely rigid. Chains and ropes are the most common solution used.

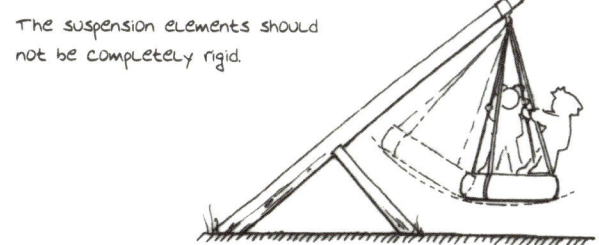

The suspension elements should not be completely rigid.

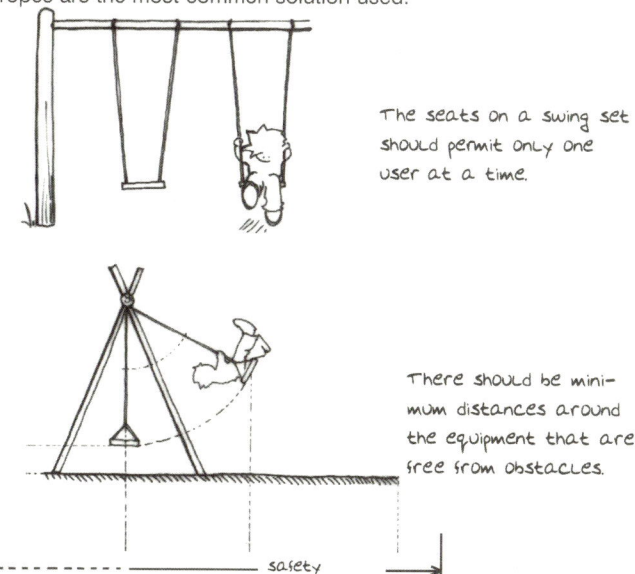

The seats on a swing set should permit only one user at a time.

There should be minimum distances around the equipment that are free from obstacles.

safety distance

Distances and surfaces

More than two swings should not hang from a single load bearing bar in order to minimize the possibility of collision when the swings are in motion. Nor should we place two harness swings for small children alongside flat swings, which are intended for bigger kids. The minimum space between seats and between a seat and an adjacent structure in order to keep them from colliding or becoming entwined vary according to different standardized regulations.

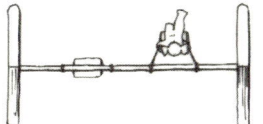

Do not install more than two swings per load bearing bar.

A surface that pads or absorbs impact should be placed beneath the seats. This surface might be synthetic or natural; non-compact materials are usually used. (For materials which pad impacts, see section 4.1)

2.4 Climbing

The activity of climbing is basic for developing a child's motor abilities; through climbing, a child learns body control, balance and coordination between arms and legs. Since climbing comes so naturally to children, elements that encourage safe climbing are recommended in a playground.

A basic installation for climbing might be made up of rigid elements, such as spatial structures or inclined surfaces with hand and foot supports. Flexible materials, such as ropes or cables, are commonly found in climbing structures. In any event, they enjoy an ample range of design possibilities and it is becoming increasingly common to see all manner of climbing structures in different playgrounds.

Climbing on rigid equipment

A simple sloped surface or low hill are elements that, by their very nature, inspire kids to climb. An easy way to equip them for this function is to incorporate supports or grips along the surface for hand and foot support. Naturally, these supports must comply with the requisites previously specified in section 3.1.

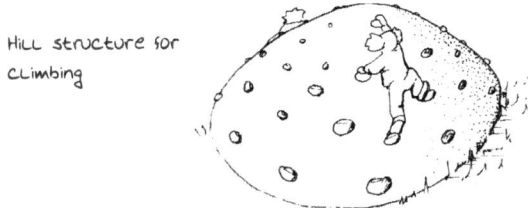

Hill structure for climbing

The classic "monkey bars" structure.

Among the available wooden or metal structures can be found the classic arch, the domed configuration of bars, or structures with horizontal ladders, bars, rings and combined elements.

Climbing posts, which children can also slide down, can be included in this category as well. The surface of these posts should be entirely free from all welding traces or discontinuities and the sliding section should be straight, that is: with no changes in direction.

Climbing on flexible equipment

Climbing on flexible elements requires greater skills of balance than with rigid structures. This makes it especially advisable to not include this type of equipment in play areas designed for very small children.

Ropes can be fastened at one or both ends. In the former case, the rope should be sufficiently rigid so as to avoid getting tangled. The weave of both simple ropes and nets should have a smooth, non-slip outer skin. Stops or fastenings are recommended in the intersection of nets in order to keep the knots from sliding. Ropes that do not have intersections should be adequately tensed so as to eliminate any risk of strangulation.

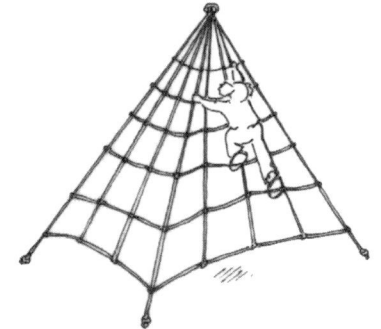

Climbing nets can be made up of ropes or galvanized cables.

Climbing ropes fastened at both ends.

The recommended diameter for ropes fastened at one end ranges between 25 and 45 mm; the rest can be anywhere from 18 to 45 mm. Braided metal cables can offer an alternative to ropes and nets. The cable should be covered with a sheath, preferably of natural fiber, although it can be synthetic. Cables should be galvanized and properly tensed so as not to buckle, unravel or knot up. These elements must be manufactured with corrosion-resistant materials.

2.5 Composite Playground Equipment

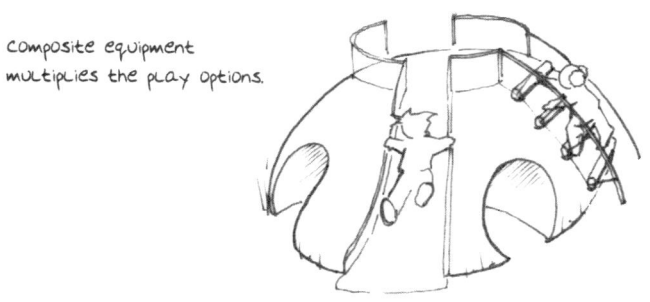

Composite equipment multiplies the play options.

The trend in today's playgrounds is to incorporate equipment which has traditionally served a single function into more complex and versatile modular structures. Indeed, when a simple seesaw or slide becomes part of a combined structure, a whole new field of possible uses is opened.

Good playground equipment should be designed for easy modification and adaptation to the different needs of the children who will be using it. As far as possible, composite structures should be equipped to offer different degrees of difficulty.

2.6 Playing with Nothing - Shapes

The imagination itself is one of a child's most important and effective instruments; which is why a given piece of equipment may seem very simple to us, but highly elaborate in the eyes of a child. We may even find it incomprehensible how that piece can come to be the favorite, even in the presence of equipment which we find to be better thought out or designed.

Any shape can serve to stimulate the imagination.

Drawings and games in the sand.

Undefined, abstract elements, such as a mound of rocks or a pile of sand, are often much more fun or interesting for children than objects that represent something concrete or specific. This is why it is recommendable to avoid realistic designs -copies of real objects such as trains, cars and houses- in playground equipment. Suggestion over representation in a playground can be much more effective.

In creating "undefined" spaces with no specific intention, we encourage experimentation and creativity and provide the opportunity for multiple uses, as many as a child's imagination can conjure. Through these undefined spaces, children can create and develop their own references.

2.7 Learning through the Senses

Elements which stimulate the senses are especially recommended for children, particularly those who suffer some form of perceptual, psychological or sensorial impairment.
Installations equipped with specific elements that encourage listening, looking, touching and even smelling can be included. Children can actively participate and interact with acoustic, visual, tactile and olfactory phenomena while at the same time learning how their own actions elicit certain responses, whose effect they may or may not understand.
Equipment designed to stimulate the senses is being seen more and more in the design of new playgrounds. The idea is to improve upon the traditional concept that playground equipment should just be fun, now incorporating educational aspects and encouraging interaction among children.

Sounds

Children love to make sound by banging on objects or rubbing them together, which is probably why we find increasingly more playgrounds featuring sound-producing equipment. The options are numerous, whether we make use of natural elements or come up with a specific system, with the end result being generally appreciated by all age groups, including adults.

The breeze blowing through bamboo.

Percussion with tubes tuned to a musical scale.

Although sounds produced naturally, for example by a breeze gently blowing through plants or the leaves of a tree, are pleasing in their own right, children will especially enjoy elements with which they can interact and experiment. A good option is to incorporate percussion systems, whistles, xylophones, and more at different points of the playground; or perhaps concave spaces, tubular and parabolic objects - anything that generates echoes, amplifications, vibrations and other effects which are often as pleasing as they are instructive.

Playing with echoes.

Watch, see, observe

In the same way that we might incorporate acoustic games, we can also design elements that play with optical effects - elements such as magnifying glasses, reflective material, prisms, kaleidoscopes, overlapping elements or color transparencies.
We can come up with an endless variety of designs for a playground, taking as inspiration experiments found in a science museum, for example; such a design would fulfill the dual function of educating and entertaining.
We often relate the sense of sight with color perception. Although it is said that children respond better to primary colors, there does not seem to be any real basis for such a statement. What is certain is that children with impaired vision find guiding references in bright colors and well defined shapes. Keeping this in mind, we will choose bright colors to stimulate visual perception, especially in those areas designed for children with difficulties, while at the same time avoiding visually overloading the rest of the playground installations.

Tools for playing with optical effects are as fun as they are educational.

Touch and texture

Experimenting with textures

We have made brief mention of the usefulness of including texture changes in paving materials in order to guide children with visual impairments. The use of different textures can also provide information about a play area, a type of apparatus or a discontinuity in the surroundings. We can establish the difference between spaces and equipment by combining various surface finishes or we can use this resource simply as another play element, encouraging a sense of discovery among small children or those with little to no eyesight, and providing a contrast between soft and hard material, dense and fluid, dry and wet, smooth and rough.

...and smell!

We do not often view the sense of smell in the same way as the other senses; although smells and their many variations are an important guiding factor for the blind or individuals with impaired vision. It might be a good idea to border paths through the park with highly fragrant plants. This olfactory and spatial system will help users find their way around the different areas of the park.

Odors can also serve as spatial references.

2.8 Building - playing with sand and mud

Children in all times and all places have naturally enjoyed playing with sand and mud, which are perfect for digging, building, sculpting, filling and emptying buckets and mixing with water. The areas set aside for this type of activity should be calm places shielded from the wind, with plenty of sun as well as partially covered by shade. It is also a good idea to keep them separated from the areas where the bigger kids play, areas where a heightened level of activity is the norm. This physical separation can be a fence, wall or shrubbery, which also imparts the feel of a calm, cozy environment.

These areas should be shielded from the wind and should include both sunny and partially shady areas.

Supervising adults should be able to keep an eye on sandboxes.

Sandboxes at different levels are a good solution for accommodating wheelchair users.

Since it is ordinarily the smallest children that most enjoy playing with sand and mud, we need to keep in mind that a supervising adult will be in attendance. Therefore, benches or some other form of seating should be included alongside these play areas.

Part of the sandbox can be adapted for playing with mud, in which case some sort of drainage system will have to be included in order to evacuate excess water. Sandy surfaces, we should remember, are not the most suitable for getting around in a wheelchair. Raised sandboxes might be a good solution for allowing all children to comfortably reach them. We can also include different types of sand, with varying thicknesses of grain, in order to provide an array of touch sensations and degrees of cohesion. The sand should be periodically removed, cleaned and renewed to keep it from hardening and to prevent minor injuries.

2.9 Splashing around - playing with water

Water offers a range of stimuli for children, from the sensations of wet and dry, to experimenting with submerged and floating objects, to changes in temperature, and so forth. Since water is a privileged feature seen only rarely in playgrounds, it might be a good idea to consider the possibility of bringing in water via artificial means - climate and resources permitting.

Learning about the properties of water.

water consumption of spouts should able to be regulated.

Streams, canals, ponds, fountains and sprinklers can all be built, thereby gaining highly attractive, not to mention educational, play areas. Water consumption and evacuation in a "wet" play zone that enjoys its own source of water should be controllable.
For safety reasons, the water should be drinkable and it should be no deeper than 35 to 40 centimeters.

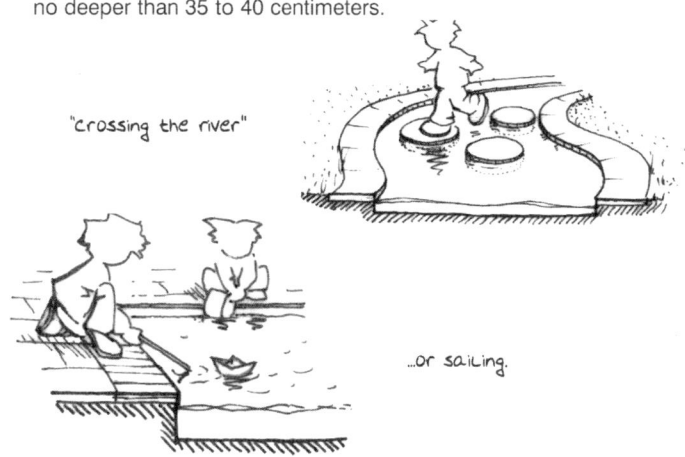

"crossing the river"

...or sailing.

To decrease the risk of slips and falls, the borders of wet zones should be well defined and constructed with non-slip material. As with sandboxes, a space where adults can sit and supervise the water zone should be included.
We mustn't forget that even the sensation of water can be imparted more or less directly via bridges and raised walkways. So, with or without water, these elements can always be incorporated into the design of a playground. The imagination will provide the river!

2.10 On wheels

If sufficient space is available, areas for skating, bicycling or even tricycling (as long as safety is ensured) are a wonderful addition to a playground or park. Mid- to large-sized bicycles, skates and other apparatuses which can reach dangerous speeds may present a danger to other park visitors. Therefore, their use should be circumscribed to specific routes and should be independent of the rest of the park. These routes can run parallel to other primary paths or independent of them; and they should be well marked.
Additionally, bike racks should be included. If the park does not include bike paths, the area for locking up the bikes should be located near the park entrance so that they can be picked up when visitors to the park leave.

Bike paths should have clearly defined boundaries.

3. Ensuring Safe Play Conditions

When we define any easy-to-do activity as "child's play", chances are we are not thinking of what really goes on in a children's playground, where bumps and falls are the norm.

It's not difficult to imagine how the youngest children are the most susceptible to having the greatest number of falls and accidents; although bigger kids also play on equipment with varying levels of difficulty - equipment whose correct or incorrect usage might involve certain risks. While most of the falls caused by a loss of balance while playing are difficult to avoid, we can dampen those falls by installing shock-absorbent paving, which is anything ranging from sand to the increasingly popular variety of synthetic materials.

Other kinds of possible accidents that may occur in a playground are those caused by the use of the equipment itself - run-ins with fixed or moveable elements, or a child getting body parts or clothes stuck in the equipment, all of which can be very dangerous. Such accidents, however, can easily be avoided. There are a series of regulations guiding the dimensions to which play equipment should be built and the minimum distances between various parts, all according to the characteristics of each given piece.

Safety issues in areas with as much activity as in a playground are complex and subject to many factors. Following are concise descriptions of some of the design considerations to bear in mind when creating playground equipment from the standpoint of preventing accidents.

3.1 Padding Impact

The most frequent accidents caused by slipping are those where there is a patch of sand and gravel spread over a smooth surface. This can be avoided by ensuring that loose paving does not spread to nearby hard or continuous ground surfaces. Puddles can also cause slips, making it necessary to install a good system of rainwater evacuation as well as a non-slip paving material.

The ground surface beneath playground equipment should be impact absorbant.

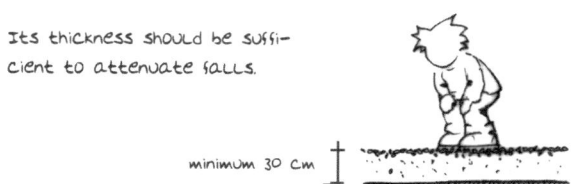

Its thickness should be sufficient to attenuate falls.

minimum 30 cm

Be careful with loose paving: it can cause slips if it spills over onto continuous paving.

The areas prone to the greatest risk of falls are those that are below or around play equipment. The most frequently used impact-absorbent materials that are spread over such ground surfaces are tree bark, wood chips, sand and gravel.
A minimum depth of 30 cm with a good drainage system is recommended for the impact absorbing properties of the material to be as efficient as possible. Additionally, in order to ensure that they continue working, they should receive continuous upkeep and periodic renovation.

While grass can also pad falls very efficiently, its degree of efficacy varies greatly according to the effects of certain weather conditions and geographical locations. Furthermore, it is subject to growth cycles and very heavy wear and tear in circulation routes and areas where the impact is constant.

Grass suffers excessive wear and tear in frequently-used areas.

Synthetic paving creates uniform surfaces and comes in a variety of colors.

Synthetic materials such as rubber or recycled foam provide the basis for smooth, homogenous surfaces (making them easily accessible for persons with reduced mobility). They can be custom designed to absorb varying levels of impact; additionally, their range of color options enriches the design. Although these materials are generally more expensive, once installed they require a minimum amount of maintenance.

3.2 Minimum Space

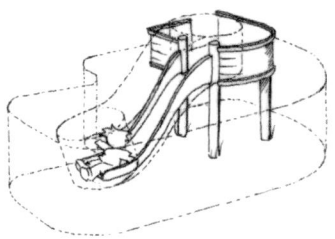

All play equipment requires some amount of space, however minimum, for its use. Such space comprises, logically, the volume occupied by the equipment itself, as well as a certain amount of the surrounding area that should be kept clear of obstacles so that the equipment may be safely and efficiently put to use.
The different regulations governing the use of playground equipment include calculations and tables for determining the safety margins necessary for each type of apparatus according to its properties and the use to which it will be put.

The area of impact

In order to minimize the risk of collisions between children, a safety zone should be created around any equipment whose use involves abrupt movements. European standards establish an obstacle-free zone, called the area of impact, of one and a half meters around the outer perimeter of a piece of raised equipment from which a child could fall.
The area of impact must remain free of obstacles up to the height of this raised point: this area is called the "fall space" and is defined as the space which might be occupied by a user in the event of falling from that height.

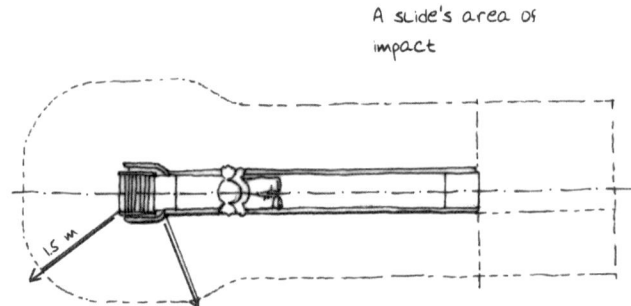

A slide's area of impact

Obstacle-free fall height

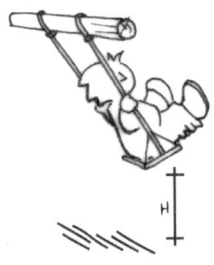

Fall height from a swing and from a platform.

The concept of the "obstacle-free fall height" is a determining factor when choosing the type of paving for the area beneath a piece of equipment. In equipment that is used while standing, the obstacle-free space will extend from the foot support to the lower surface. If the equipment is used while sitting, the space is that between the seat and the lower surface; in pieces from which the user hangs, from the hand support to the lower surface.
In order to determine the obstacle-free fall height we must consider the possible movement of the equipment as well as its users. By defining such concepts as "area of impact" or "fall height" we can begin to form an idea of the necessary parameters for ensuring that a play area is safe and that the risk of accidents caused by the equipment is minimized.

3.3 Protection Against Getting Stuck

Another possible playground danger is that children may get a body part or a piece of clothing stuck in openings that are too small or narrow. Again, there are standardized regulations guiding the design and dimensional requisites for minimizing this risk.

In general, elements in which body parts or clothing might get stuck are those which feature a closed perimeter, such as tunnel slides,

Open-perimeter opening... ...and closed perimeter.

Be careful with moveable parts.

open tubes and nets, as well as apparatuses with an open perimeter, amongst which are grooves, cracks and V-shaped openings.

Moveable parts on playground equipment are also liable to cause entrapment, specifically between the moving parts and the ground, which is why we must respect the minimum safety distances for the equipment as stipulated in the corresponding regulations.

Getting the head or neck stuck

The head can get stuck in openings that are intended to be entered head first as well as those where the child enters feet first. Closed perimeter openings, slits, sharp angles, flexible elements (ropes, chains, nets), openings in fences and railings can all cause entrapment of the head and neck, which is why it is crucial to ensure the appropriate dimensions when designing them.

It is crucial to ensure the suitable dimensions in the design of playground equipment.

Getting the extremities stuck

The ends of tubes should be closed.

Careful with the feet...

Let's turn our attention to those openings in which fingers might get stuck while the rest of the body is in motion, a situation that can occur when a child is sliding or swinging.

Entrapment of fingers and hands can also be caused by the open ends of tubes or pipes. We should therefore make sure that they are sealed off and that the seal cannot be removed without the use of tools.

In the event that a child has one or more extremities trapped in a raised or inclined point, a possible fall in this position could cause very serious injuries. We should eliminate this risk by paying special attention to the dimensions of those rigid openings and closed perimeter openings on surfaces where children can run or climb, especially if they are raised or inclined.

design for fun:
playspaces

design for fun:
playspaces

Index

7	Introduction	72	EDAW Gateway Science School Courtyard
8	Rehwaldt Landschaftsarchitekten Playing Hill	76	Taylor Cullity Lethlean & Mary Jeavons The Quarries
16	Thread Collective Sydney's Playground	82	Mitsuru Senda + Environment Design Institute Hamamatsu Science Museum
22	PREC Institute Inc. Tsujido Seaside Park	88	Isabelle Devin & Catherine Rannou Parc Astérix
28	Paddy Burton Sound Sculptures	100	EDAW Ross's Landing Park and Plaza
34	Taylor Cullity Lethlean MLC Junior School	104	Helle Nebelong Murergaarden
42	architectureisfun, Inc. CCM	112	PREC Institute Inc. Tochigi Wanpaku Park
48	Mitsuru Senda + Environment Design Institute Circular Play Structure	118	Centerbrook Stepping Stones Museum
52	KOMPAN Magna Science Adventure Centre	126	Marinela S. de Lerdo de Tejada - Maribel Ibarra Papalote Childrens Museum
56	Topotek 1 Playground Niebuhrstrasse	136	Taylor Cullity Lethlean Springthorpe Playground
62	Kijo Rokkaku Architect & Associates Kankaku Museum	142	Interplay Design & Manufacturing, Inc. Play Structure

152	Patricia Johanson **Fair Park Lagoon**		226	architectureisfun, Inc. **Go Green! - Environmental Play**
160	Mitsuru Senda + Environment Design Institute **Aichi Children's Center**		228	Mitsuru Senda + Environment Design Institute **Kainan Wanpaku Park**
166	Kompan **Parque de la Ribera**		232	ZEE **Kinder Museum / Zoom Ocean**
176	Northern Light CoDesign **Eureka! SoundSpace**		238	architectureisfun, Inc. **Louisville Science Center Fit Project**
186	Atsugi C.E.D. & Tokio LAndsc. Architects Inc. **Wooden Playthings**		242	Mitsuru Senda + Environment Design Institute **Toyama Children's Center**
190	architectureisfun, Inc. **DuPage Children's Museum**		250	architectureisfun, Inc. **The Granger Children's Ministry**
198	Taylor Cullity Lethlean & Mary Jeavons **Tea Tree Gully**		256	Martirià Figueras **Floreix**
202	Kaiser & Kühne **Large Playground**		264	Topotek 1 **Castle Park: temporary playground**
206	Richard Dattner & Partners Architects PC **Central Park Playgrounds**			
210	PREC Institute Inc. **Funabashi Wanpaku Park**			
216	Rehwalat Landschaftsarchitekten **Playground Pelzmühle Chemnitz**			

Introduction

We tend to view the activity of playing as a non-serious pursuit -- kids' stuff -- with neither transcendence nor goal. We should remember, however, how much we ourselves learned during our earliest years while playing. Playing and learning are crucial for a child's development; and providing good play opportunities is a way to directly contribute to achieving this fundamental goal in the first stages of life.

From around the age of two onward, children spend more and more time playing, either alone or with adults at first and, later, with other children. Playing comes naturally; it forms part of children's daily activities and contributes to their physical, mental and emotional growth from the very start.

Not only do children release energy and develop motor skills, balance and coordination through play, but they also forge their personalities through social activities while stimulating creativity, the capacity to reason and language skills. Through play, children create custom-made realities and experiences. They learn to resolve problematic situations, confront new challenges and set their sights on new goals, all of which foments their capacity to organize, plan and make decisions. Play activities, therefore, are invaluable "dress rehearsals" for their future lives.

Playing Hill   Rehwaldt Landschaftsarchitekten

Burghausen, Germany   photographs: Rehwaldt Landschaftsarchitekten

An urban park was developed in Burghausen Neustadt, comprising the main area of the 2004 state garden show. Three different borderlines delimit a wide meadow area and mark the boundaries of the park. Zones are indicated through the different uses and configurations within this fluid space. Their character corresponds with the adjacent residential areas, each having its own formal character.
Shortly after entering the park a vast view opens up over the meadow. Reticular paths intersect the park, making direct connections between the city center and the adjacent residential areas.
In the northern part the Spielgebirge (playing hill) is the space's defining element. The peculiar "Micro-Alps" area symbolizes the yearning for the real massif and is a playground for all ages. The hilltops and valleys accommodate different playing alternatives: water valley, climbing canyon, sand troughs and slide. A viewpoint on the "summit" provides a perfect view of the park.

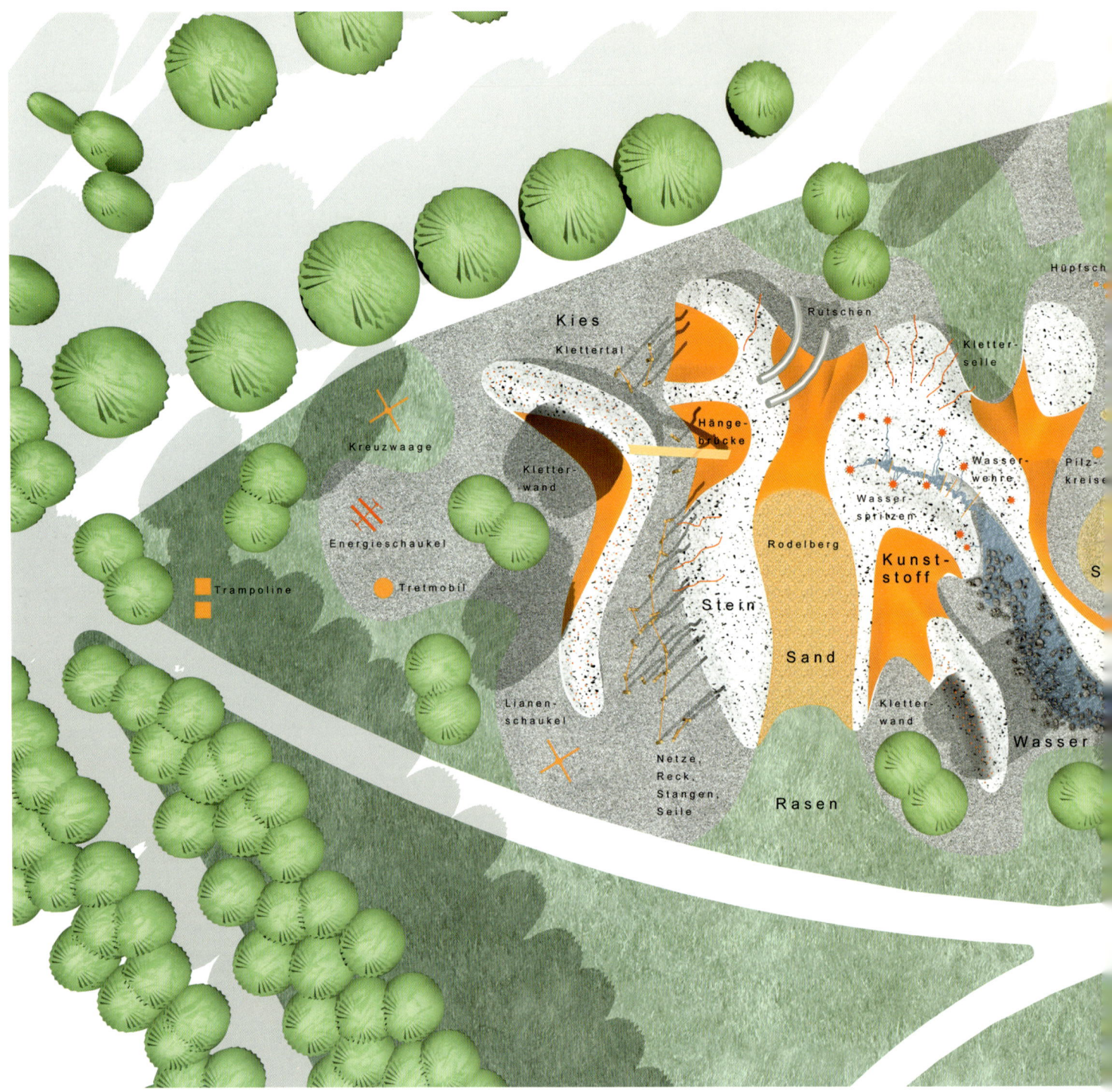

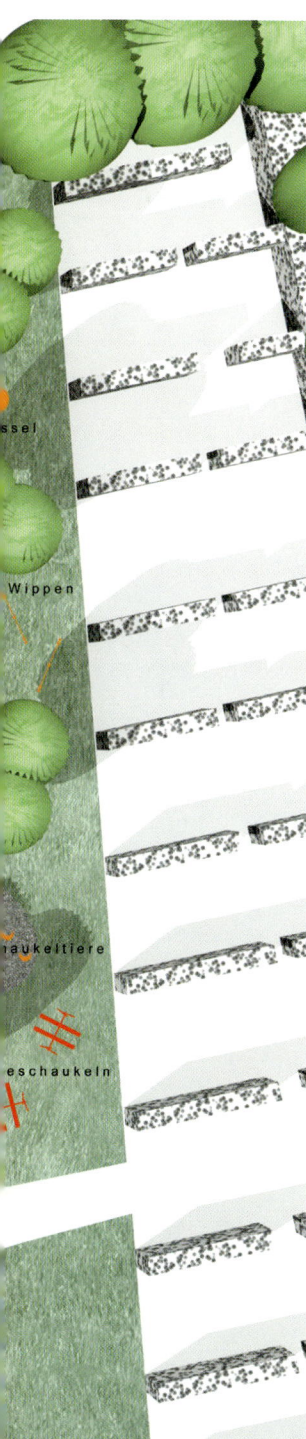

© Fa. Corocord, Berlin

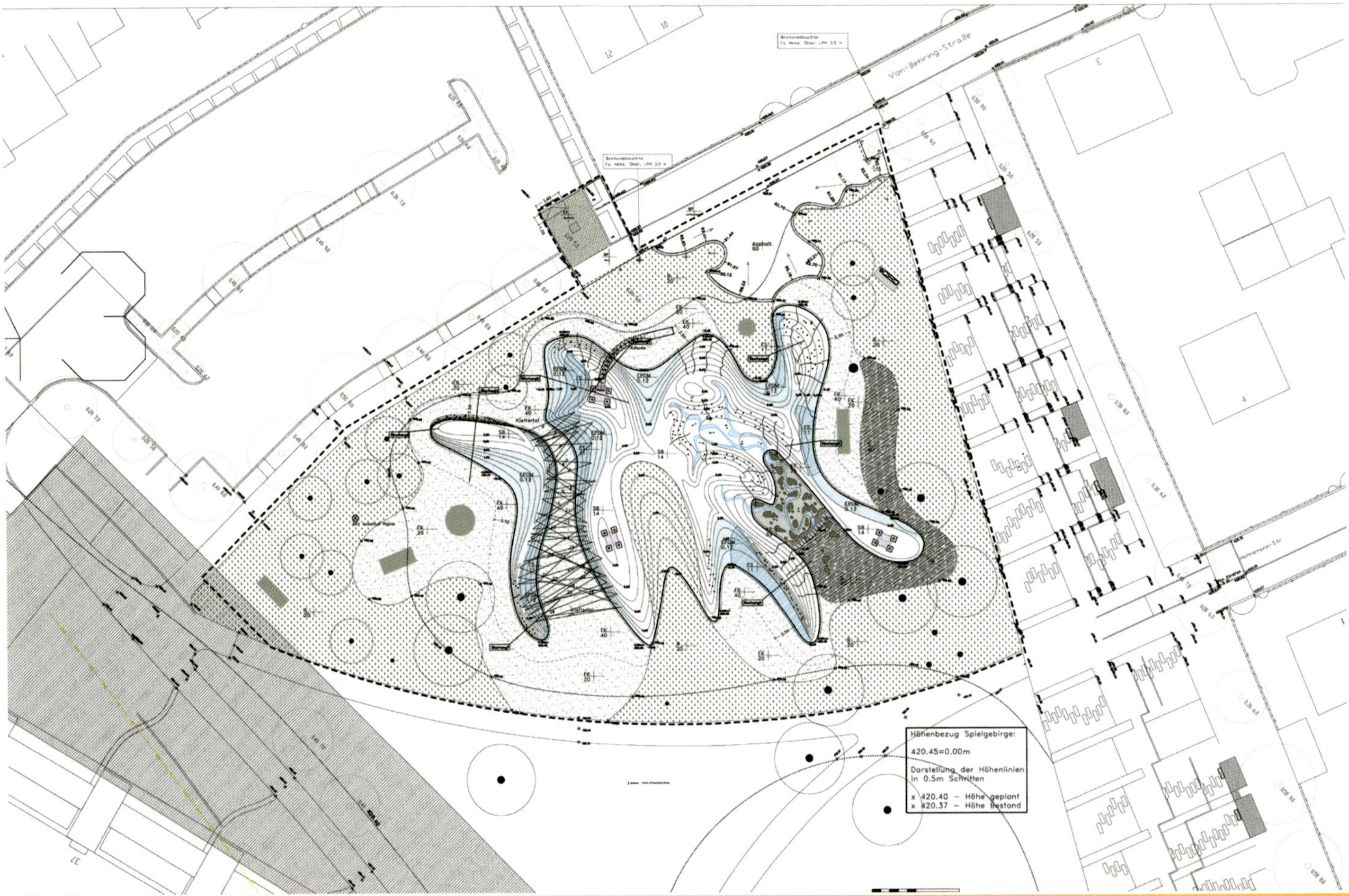
Von-Behring-Straße
Höhenbezug Spielgebirge:
420.45=0.00m
Darstellung der Höhenlinien in 0.5m Schritten
x 420.40 – Höhe geplant
x 420.37 – Höhe Bestand

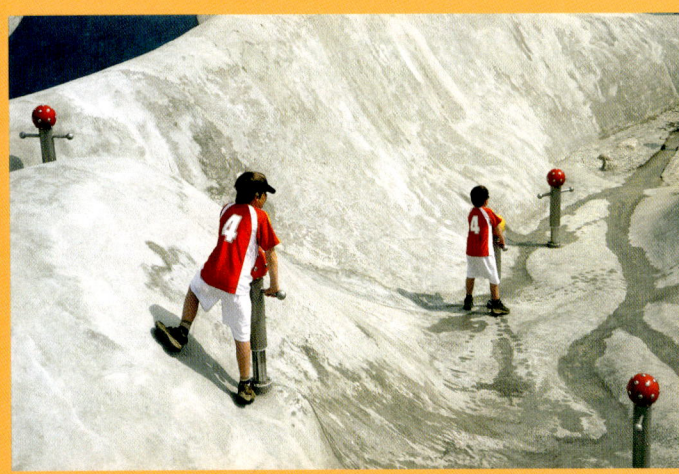

Sydney's Playground
Thread Collective

New York, USA

photographs: Noah Sheldon

A vibrant orange tunnel creates a sense of instant excitement as one enters the indoor playground and visually frames the open play area and the new mezzanine. Mesh fabric panels with orange clouds wrap half of the tunnel, introducing the idea that the city outside has been brought inside, while also preserving a sense of transparency in the space. A toy store and locker area are located on either side of the tunnel.

A child-scaled city with layered spaces and an integrated tree house dominates one side of the open play space. Real tree trunks rise from the floor to the ceiling with abstract canopies of mesh fabric to provide a sense of enclosure at the two raised platforms. While familiar as a streetscape, including floor materials that suggest grass and sidewalks, the space maintains a level of abstraction consistent with current theories of child play – abstraction allows the children more room to imagine. Beyond the city are a small toddler area and sandbox.

Facing the city, bench seating and a café offer places for adults to gather, socialize, and watch the children at play. The countertop is removable, transforming the raised area of the café into a stage for special events – platforms in front of the city serve as additional seating.

An enclosed room tucked under the new mezzanine is designed for mothers with children under 6 months. Wrapped with carpet, with walls painted a warm dark red, the space envelopes one immediately, creating a distinct feel from the rest of the play area. Black and white mobiles hang at various heights for the newborns, who can only see tones in black, white, and red.

Stairs lead to an open walkway on the mezzanine, from which one can view the entire space. The walkway provides access to the party room, which is one large space that can be converted into two rooms with a moveable partition.

Designed for both children under 5 and their adult friends, Sydney's Playground occupies the ground floor of a late 19th century warehouse building in the Tribeca neighborhood in New York City.

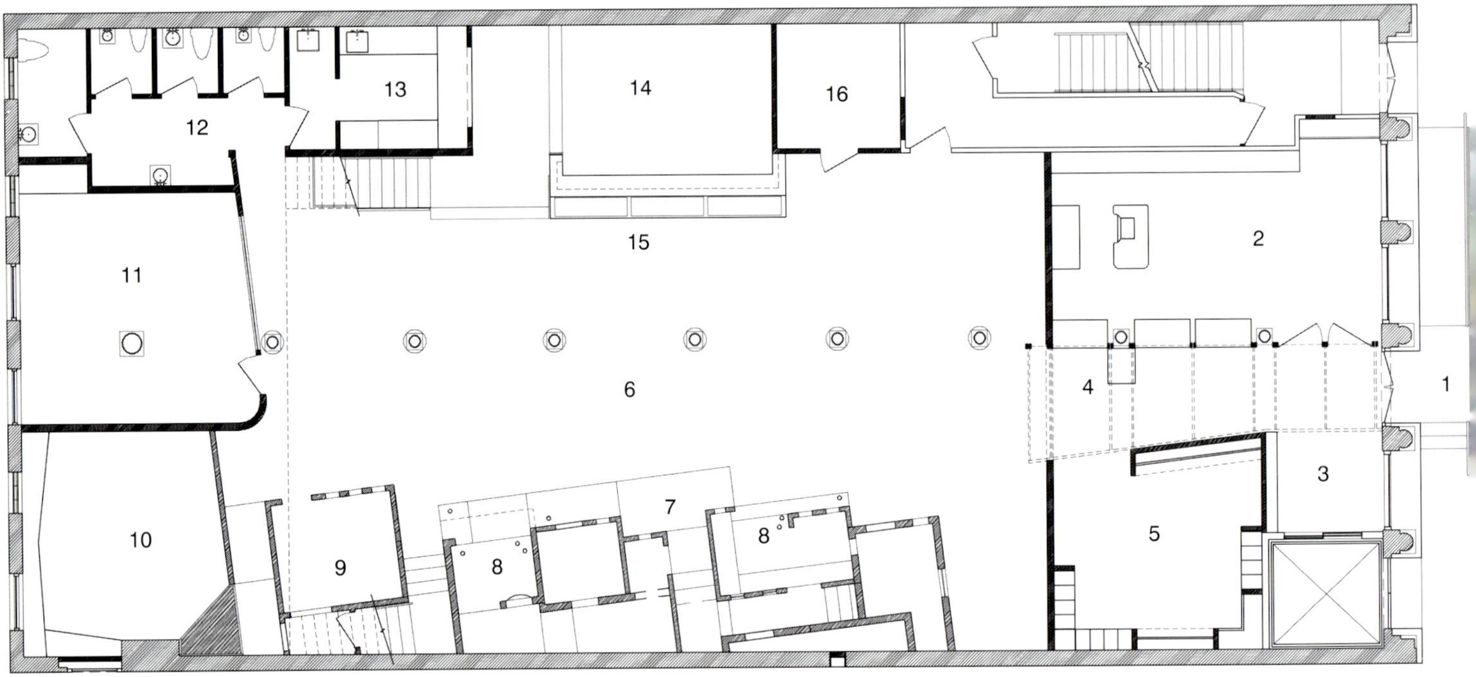

Ground floor

1. Entrance
2. Toy store
3. Lobby
4. Tunnel
5. Locker area
6. Open play area
7. Climbing city
8. Trees
9. Toddler area
10. Sandbox
11. Newborn area
12. Changing area - WC
13. Cafe pantry
14. Cafe seating
15. Play area seating
16. Mechanical

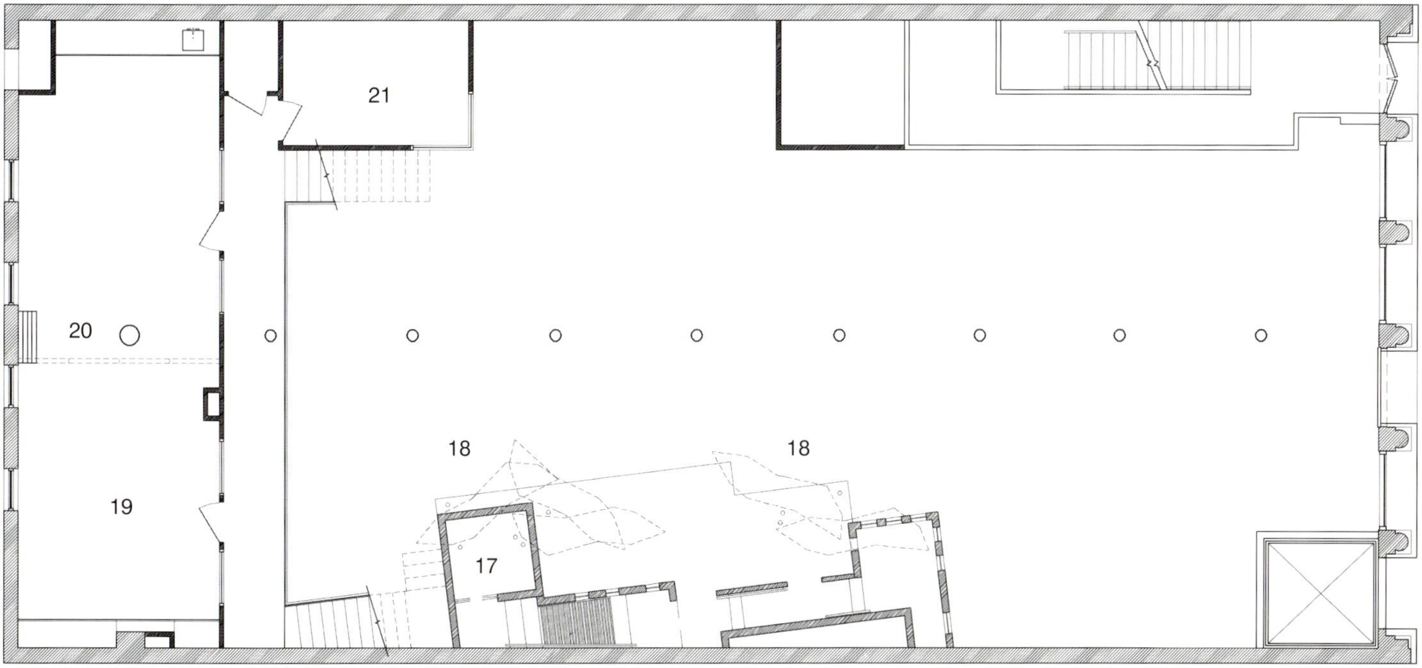

Mezzanine

17. Upper platform
18. Canopies
19. Party room
20. Movable partition
21. Office

Tsujido Seaside Park

PREC Institute Inc.

Fujisawa City, Kanagawa Prefecture, Japan

photographs: Katsuomi Wada

To make the best use of the features of the site's seaside location, its three natural resources – sea, breezes and light – were worked together in the landscape design of the park.

The playground of the park is roughly divided into three areas. The Vehicle Riding Area provides ample space for children to ride around on bicycles and skates.

The Lawn Area is a simple field overlooking the sea where children can fly kites, play ball games or invent any number of games. A generally recreational, festive atmosphere has been achieved in this section by the monument stirring in the wind, the pond and fountain, the palm-lined promenade and the vibrancy of the flowers.

Finally, the Water Adventure Area includes a variety of play equipment and installations, such as a spiral slide, a tide pool and a wave pool.

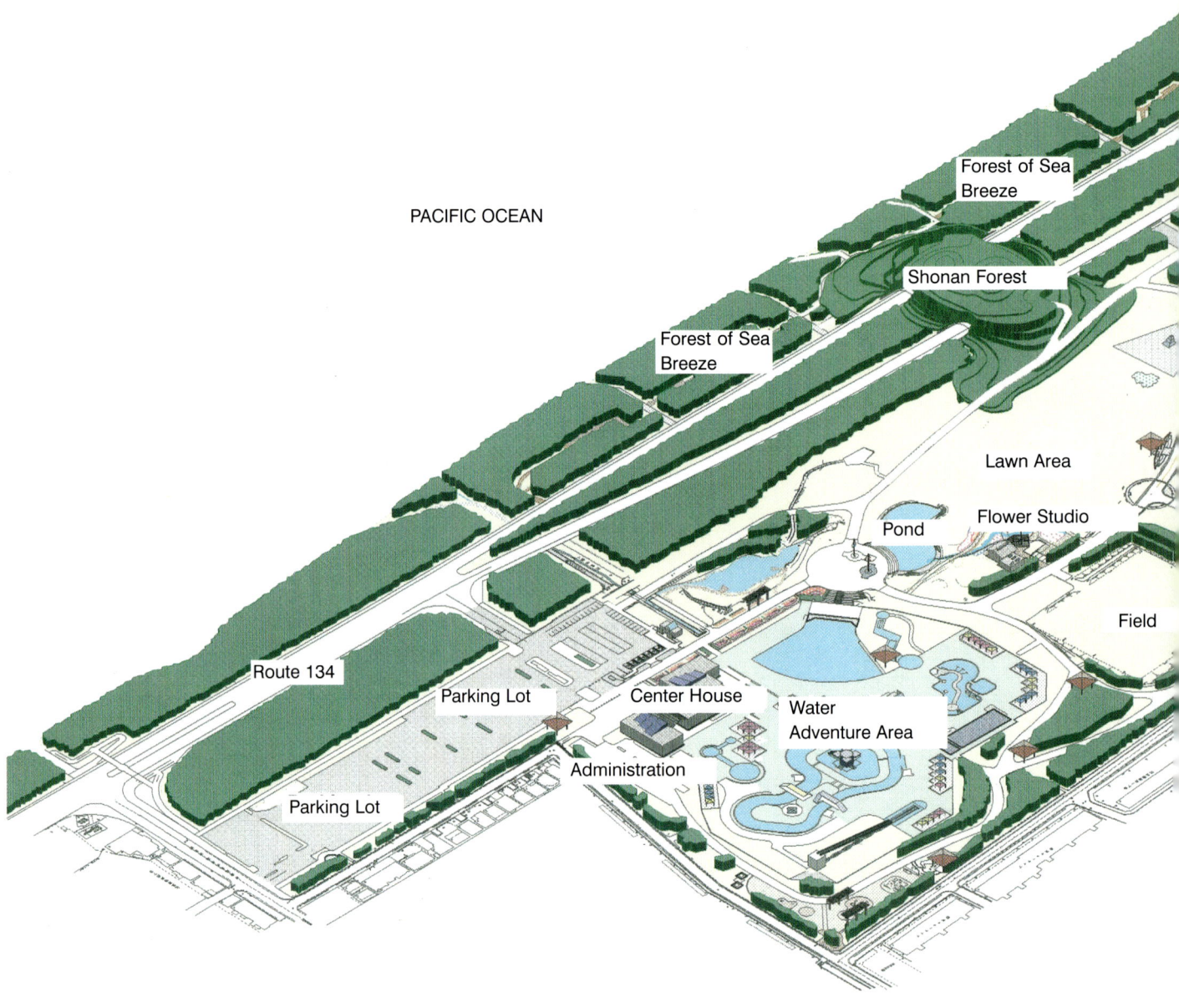

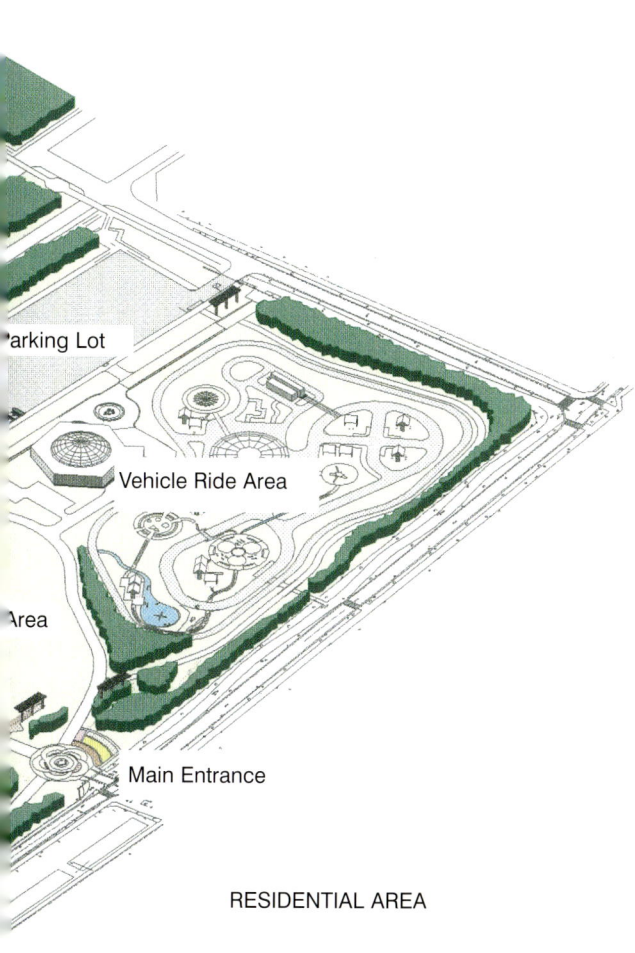

Parking Lot

Vehicle Ride Area

Area

Main Entrance

RESIDENTIAL AREA

Sound Sculptures (tubular bells, slit drums)

Paddy Burton

photographs: Contributed by Paddy Burton

The designer and builder of these unique sound structures, Paddy Burton, first began creating them in the early 1990s while "musician in residence" for the City of Edinburgh District Council, which requested a number of outdoor musical play installations for parks in the city.

These sculptures are called "slit drums" and are logs which have chainsaw-cut slits that become musical notes. The instrument can then be played with chunky hardwood sticks by just one person or groups of up to six people. The underlying aim of these drums is to encourage fun atmospheres for socializing, while also creating durable resources for public spaces. The artist believes in the therapeutic benefits of drumming for promoting harmony and cooperation; and drumming in groups is an excellent way of enhancing communication between players.

The pieces are generally built from native hardwood – oak, beech or yew, for example – and they are often commissioned by forestry or countryside organizations. They are often composed on site in geometric arrangements and the ends of the logs might sometimes be sculpted into animal shapes.

MLC Junior School

Taylor Cullity Lethlean

Melbourne, Australia

photographs: Taylor Cullity Lethlean

A new playground has recently been created as part of the Methodist Ladies College's new junior school development. The project creates a maximum of interest for the 7 to 8 year olds within a confined site by utilizing an existing change of level as a major play feature.

Composed within the image of an eroding sand dune, a sequence of active, social and exploratory play elements are integrated into the sculptural walls. Constructed of rendered Gunite walls, the project challenges pre-conceived notions of what is a safe and appropriate playground material. The hardness of concrete contrasts with the softness of the shapes and tones that make them seem almost edible. Yet safety is guaranteed. A large pergola shields the space and accentuates the refuge-like aspect conferred by the interior and perimetral walls.

Slides, dance steps, spiral stairs, climbing nets and ramps allow a new way to enter the schoolyard every day.

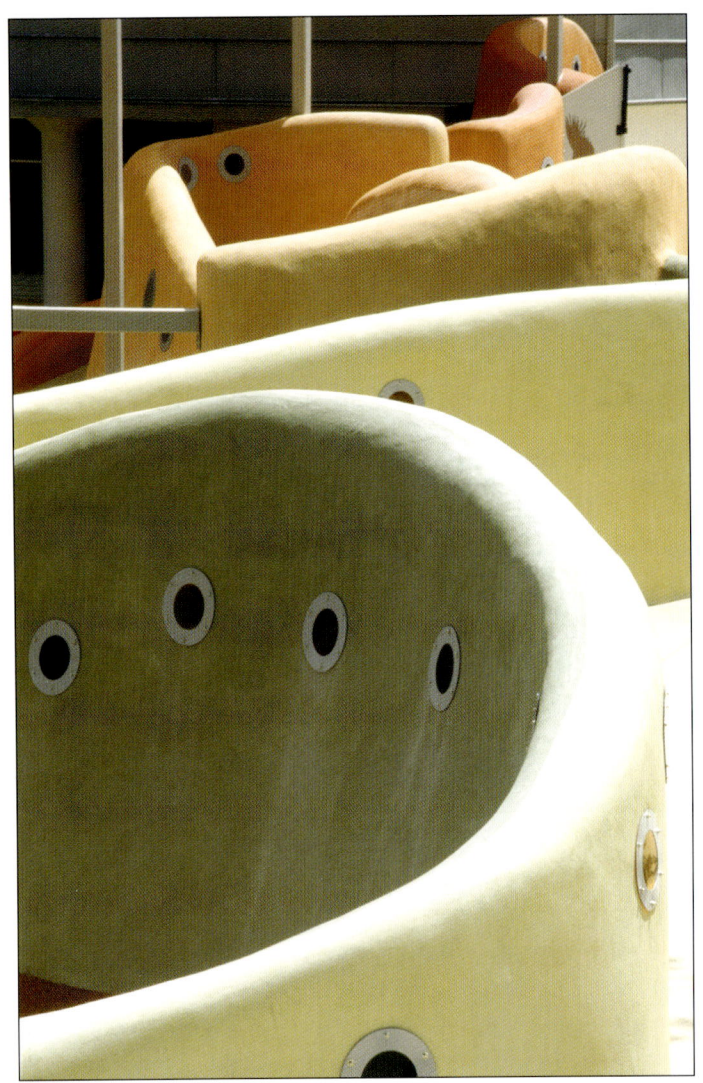

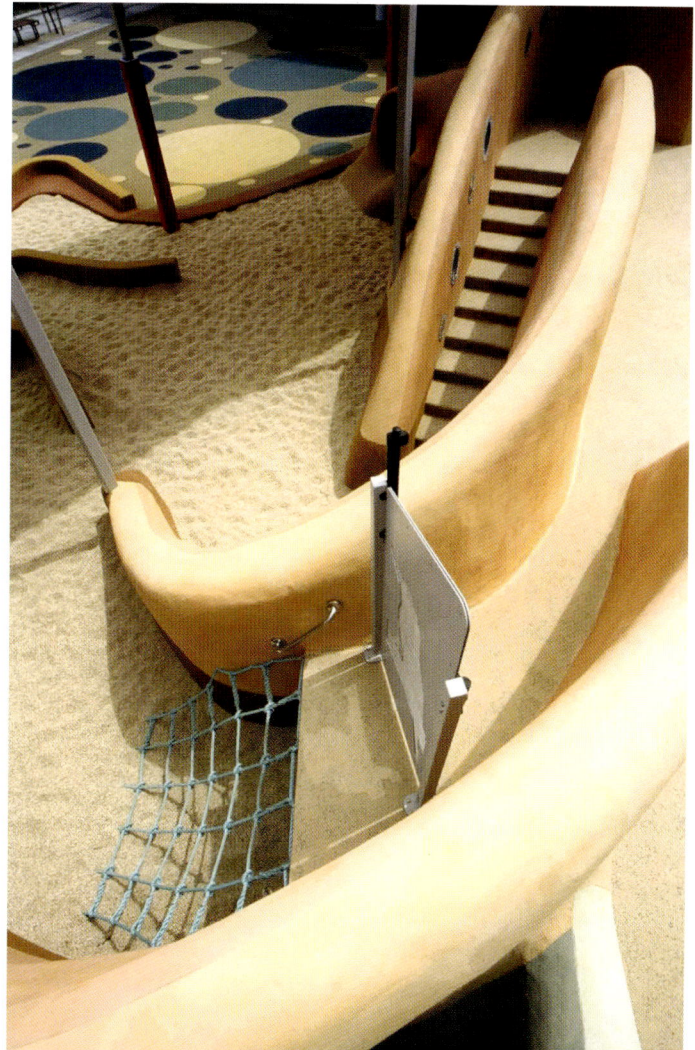

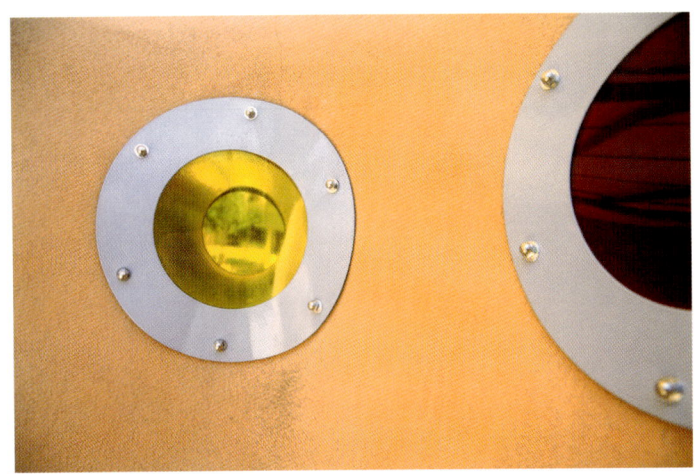

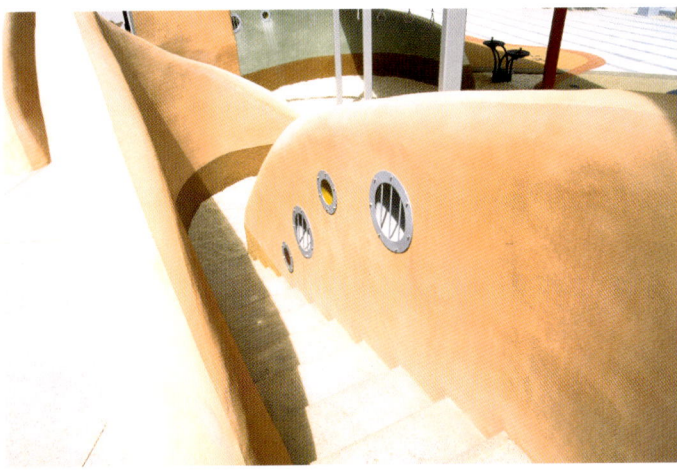

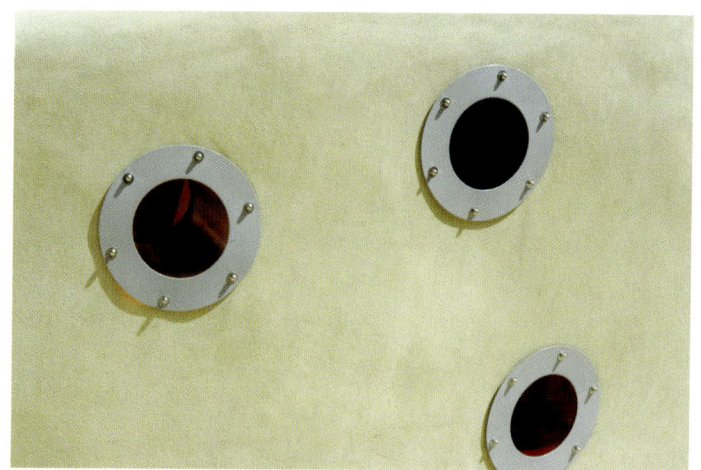

CCM: Stinking Truth about Garbage and Playmaze

architectureisfun, Inc.

Chicago, Illinois, USA

photographs: Doug Snower

A fanciful miniature metropolis, Playmaze encourages a child's imagination through cognitive, social, and physical skills in a context-rich and integrated environment. Using the urban context as a theme, Playmaze offers visitors at the Chicago Children's Museum at Navy Pier a 1500-square-foot space dedicated to early childhood development.

Specially designed for children up to six years of age and their caregivers, Playmaze is designed as a colorful city teeming with activity and opportunities for fun and learning. Exploring familiar places and everyday objects, the exhibits demystify daily experiences from which children are usually sheltered. Incorporating role-playing and interaction with adults, Playmaze assists children in their development of a sense of ownership, attachment, security, and place identity to the world around them.

The city in movement, work, play, and rest beckons as the child and caregiver enter through a controlled gate expressing the uniqueness of the space. Toddlers can drive a replica of a city bus, or change the tires and license plates on the Playmaze automobile. Donning waterproof smocks, they can use squeegees at the Car Wash, or pump gas and rebuild a motor to see how pieces fit together at the Gas Station.

A secure Tot Lot with a "peek-a-boo" bench offers more privacy and shelter from the bustle of activity. Play stations, such as a bakery fully stocked for baking, selling, and packaging, offer opportunities for "city work" and adventure using a broad range of sensory perceptions (water play at the car wash, kneading dough at the kitchen).

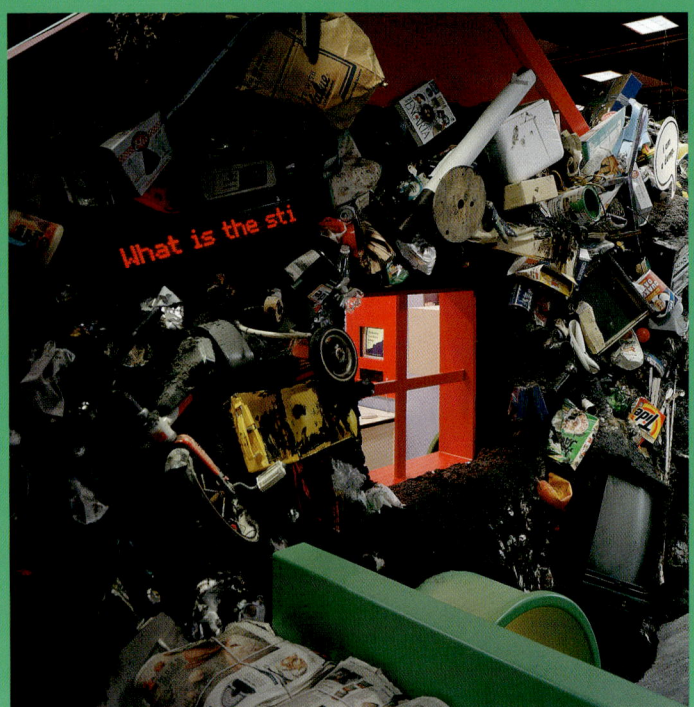

Via stimulating imagery and interactive elements, The Stinking Truth About Garbage engages children and teaches them responsibility for our world. Practical solutions to serious problems are introduced through two families with contrasting environmental attitudes. Each family's house is a small pavilion representative of a typical home from a child's perspective. The homes are physically and symbolically tied together with a transitional volume of garbage that makes a metamorphous link from dump to sanitary landfill to reclaimed landfill. These iconographic elements provide an architecturally unconventional spatial environment for visitors to explore and crawl through as they discover "The Stinking Truth About Garbage." The exhibit is a huge piece of recycled art and architecture, emphasized by the incorporation of commissioned art as well as the art that is created by children in the Re-Creation Station portion of the exhibit. Children test their newfound environmental knowledge on an interactive computer program designed by the architect.

Circular Play Structure

Mitsuru Senda + Environment Design Institute

Matsumoto, Nagano, Japan

photographs: Mitsumasa Fujitsuka

This is the children's pavilion for the Shinshu Expo held in the city of Matsumoto. It is an architectural play structure that provides numerous possibilities for inventing games, learning and active physical play for children of all ages, all encompassed within a single circular unit with a circumference of eighty meters.

It is three stories high and made mostly of wood, with steel serving as additional structural support.

This "circular play structure" is also a nature discovery play station where children can hear the sounds of the wind or birds singing while playing, view an open planetarium, and experience the four seasons in Matsumoto.

Originally intended as a temporary structure, it was greeted with such enthusiasm that it was left as a permanent playground after its original use – the Expo – had come to an end.

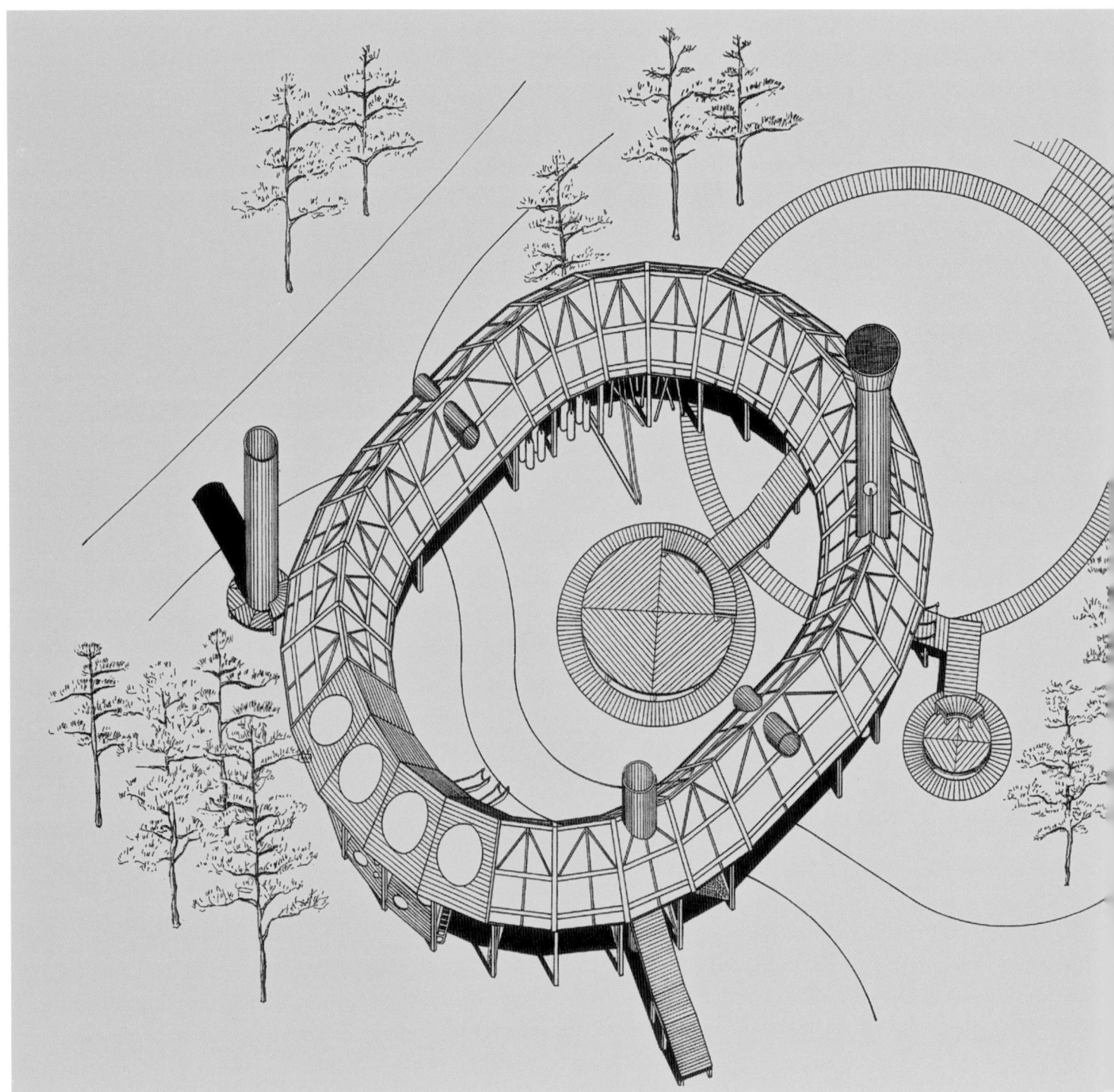

Magna Science Adventure Centre

Kompan

Rotherham, UK photographs: contributed by Kompan

Magna is set in an old steelworks covering 32 acres of land. The site that had been chosen for the play area is one of the first things visitors see as they approach the entrance. So, as well as being appealing and functional, the play area had to be visually striking if it was not to be dwarfed by its surroundings.

Anita De Brouwer, Magna's education manager in the first years of the playground's existence, was closely involved with the adventure play area from its original conception: "One of the key aims at Magna is to bring science to life and make it relevant and interesting. From the outset, we wanted the outdoor adventure play area to reflect and extend the themes that are explored through the indoor exhibitions. Now we've been open a year the play area has proved to be even better than we ever expected or hoped for!" So much so that Anita regularly hosts groups from schools and colleges who use the adventure playground as a basis for teaching and practical lessons in design.

The award-winning playground design developed by KOMPAN mirrors the elemental themes of earth, air, fire and water that run through the whole of the Magna Centre, allowing children to experience the concepts in a playful way. The design of the area aims at children of different ages with a stimulating journey of discovery through the four different themes. This was achieved by innovative use of equipment in each of four zones representing the four elements.

The air zone, for example, includes parabolic speaking dishes that enable children to speak to each other across a picnic area and a pentagonal five-way swing that allows children to almost meet in the middle as they swing together through the air. The zone also has a large spinning net, a cable way and a large high climbing area, all of which pick up different facets of the air theme through play.

Other zones include equipment such as a 160-square-meter castle, providing a play environment for younger children that encourages family participation, and the award winning Arcturus Constellation from the GALAXY range. This has a distinct sculptural form with elements designed to appeal to older children's imagination and abilities.

With up to 1000 children visiting Magna each day, it is also important that the playground has enough interest and content to engage very large numbers of children at the same time. Consequently, the mix of equipment is designed to appeal to children of all ages and abilities, with an emphasis on pieces that do not demand any lining up.

As Anita points out, "with college pupils using it as part of their curriculum, the area has a very broad appeal." So it may be that, as well as providing an award-winning environment for today's children, KOMPAN's adventure playground at Magna is also inspiring the award-winning playground designers of the future.

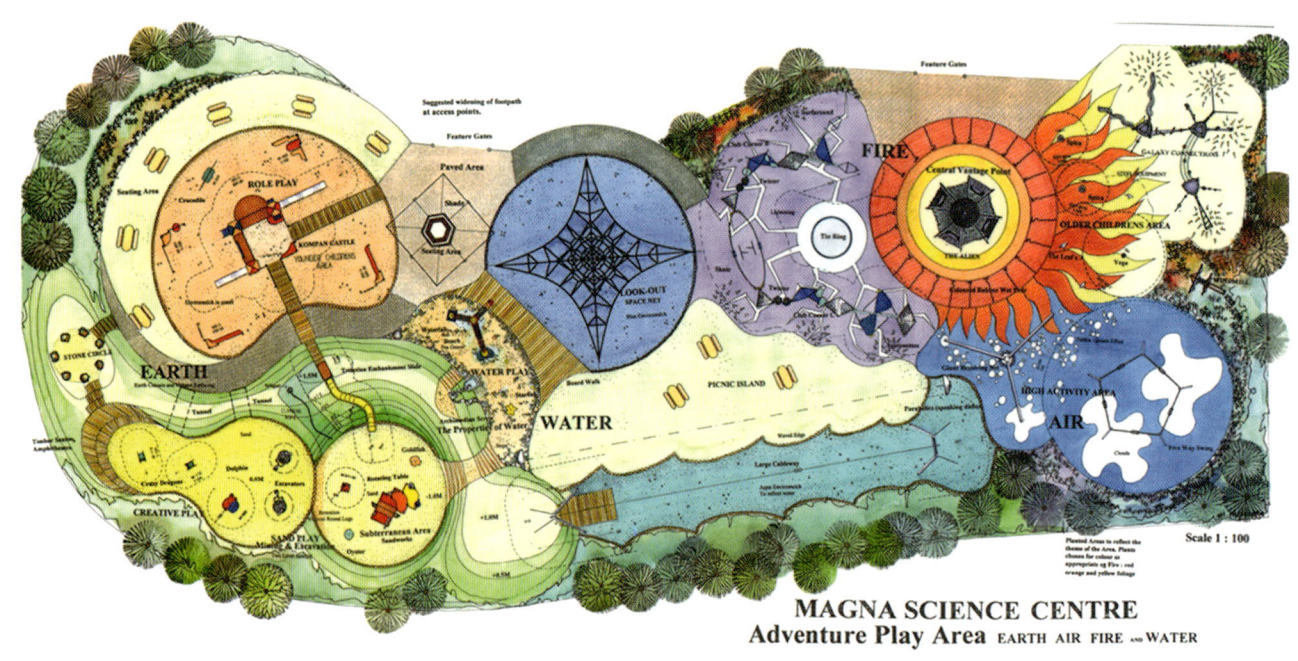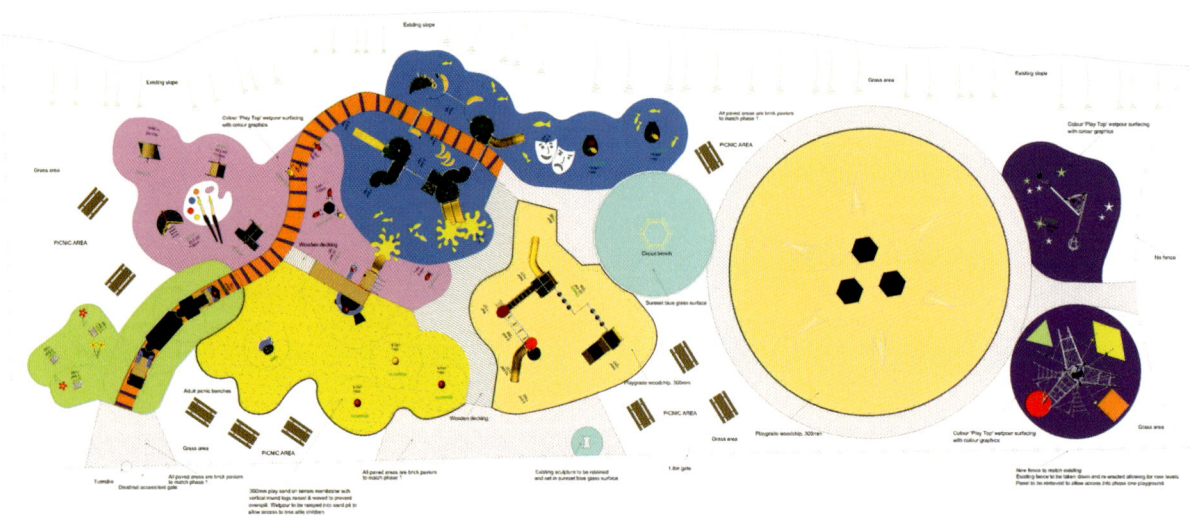

Playground Niebuhrstrasse
Topotek 1

Charlottenburg, Berlin, Germany

photographs: Hanns Joosten

In the inner city of West-Berlin, despite standard rules and regulations, an awkward site has been transformed into an unusual meeting point which is an invitation to discover new ways of playing games. The fact that it is sunken 1,5m into the ground gives it the appearance of a concise playbox rather than a regular playground. The dimensions of the space are below standard regulation and the outline of its perimeter is not in accordance with the norms of sports as we know them, thereby making the creation of new sets of rules imperative. Enhancing creativity of unconventional variants of sport became one of the themes of the project. The flooring material extends beyond the horizontal surface of the space, rising to cover its vertical sides as well. A wall made of precast concrete curves defines a 'stand' at one end of the space, marking a vertical limit that reaches towards the sky. The tall fence of spiraling wire mesh has been but up in two layers to create a stimulating moiré effect.

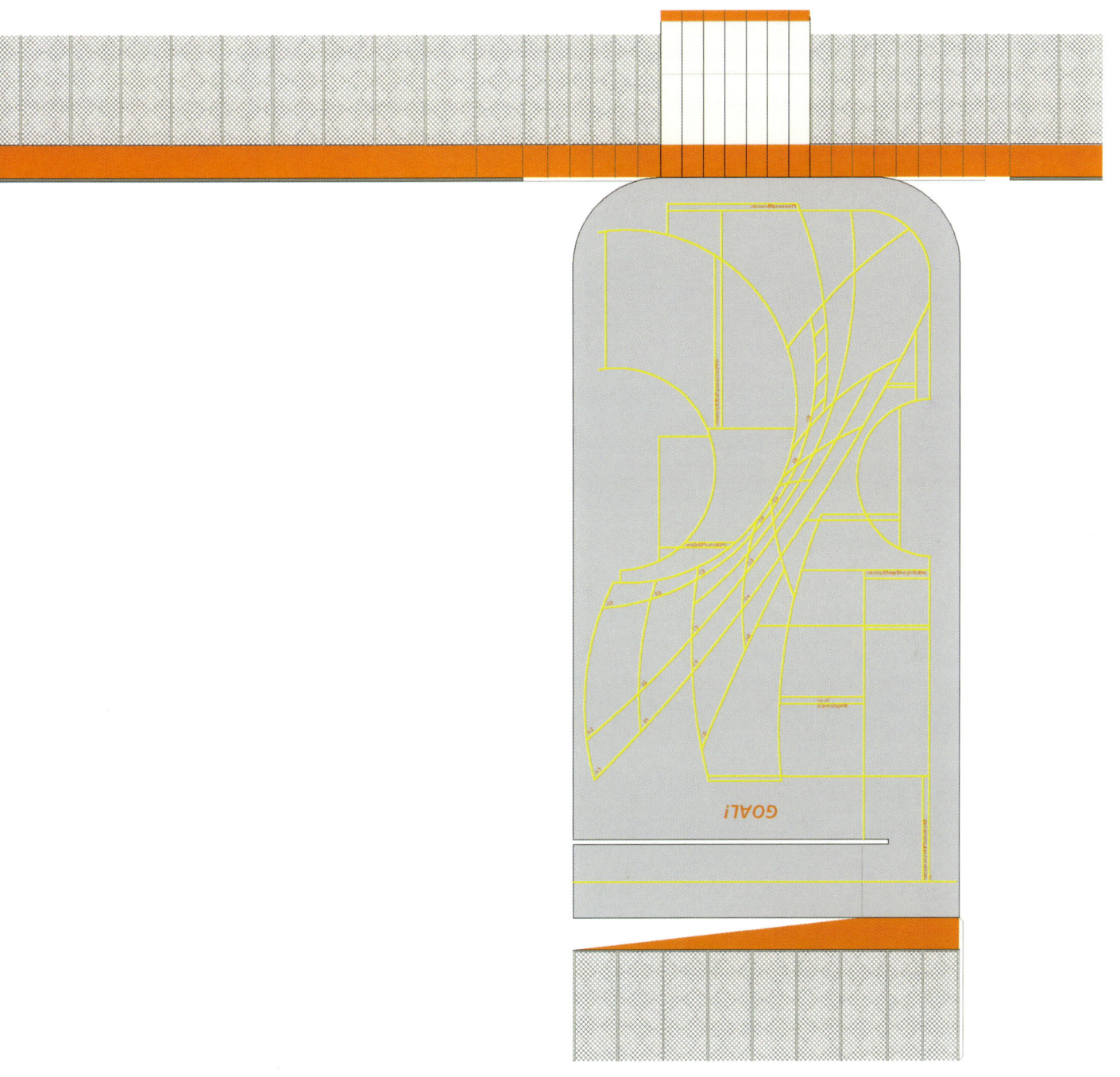

Kankaku Museum

Kijo Rokkaku Architect & Associates

Iwadeyama Town, Japan

photographs: contributed by Kijo Rokkaku

Visitors' senses are stimulated both in mind and body at Kankaku Museum (the Sense Museum). The building, encompassing nearly 2000 square meters of floor space, is structured around an oval-shaped plaza, which includes a grassy area that serves as a sort of front yard for the museum.

The interior has been roughly divided into three blocks: the dialogue zone, the monologue zone and the traverse zone.

The aim of the "dialogue zone" is to stimulate the physical senses. Here, visitors can touch the exhibit and the surrounding space, stimulating the imagination and creating a virtual conversation (the "dialogue").

The monologue zone is geared toward the "mental" senses, with meditation as a central theme. The idea here is to tune out visitors' everyday senses and foster peace of mind and a sense of new discovery.

The traverse zone connects the dialogue zone and the monologue zone and has two routes: go and return. The "going" path subjects visitors to alternating patches of darkness and light as they walk through a thick forest, open air and forest again. The "return" path leads through a water-themed space complete with cascades.

闇の世界って何だろう。何ないに見るのか
地上においては光を遮断するか、目をつぶれば...
光を失えば距離感が無くなり、目をつぶれば
心と頭の中は無限の闇が開かれる。
闇の世界でうすかに感じることができら
ひとつはその存在の姿と想像するだろう
ひとつは失われた方向性をさぐるだろう
ひとつはその領域や空間をたどるだろう
そして、それらは不安から
安心へとしるだろうかもしれ
ない。闇は日常と言う
ことで恐怖 不安を
とじよう世界だが、心付かな
い。お頭の活動が休まるとき
がやってくる、寝りにつく、体息の
自然、夢の世界が開かれていく
夢は経験と語た言語。
極楽、熱怖 死のいりみだれ
た世界だろう。そこには日常
越えなれる路線、映像が
不思議をつくりだされていく。

実在ある空間風景で、それもほんのわずか
な時間での体験で、どうすれば......
研 この空間は光の少ない時間にしたところ
全体は黒く塗りこめられている。
壁は細い...線がクモの巣のようにあるいは、紙?
きさな線の形で描かれ分けられている。
床もその線路の連続で分割され、部分に
鏡や、時々光る蛍光のライトがしくまれている。
天井から壁には実在の糸(ほをロープリがいい)
クモの巣のように張られていて、人が触れる
何かしらには全体がゆれる。不動の
壁の鏡と違合して空間にゆがみが
起る。ライトはブラックライトが主体で
時折床下の縁から色の光がほん
の少し光る。フラッシュもあるか?
糸は自らゆれるか全糸を見としてもよ
か...
音(電音は)ツッカーの?ひびきを
とりいれ、コンコン、コッコツ、
キンキン、カンカン、
地の中の世界はみえない。乱音の中を透視で
色自由に楽しむと、そこはどんな世界だろう。

Open Heart Museum　Darkspace Project　　　　8. SEP. 1998

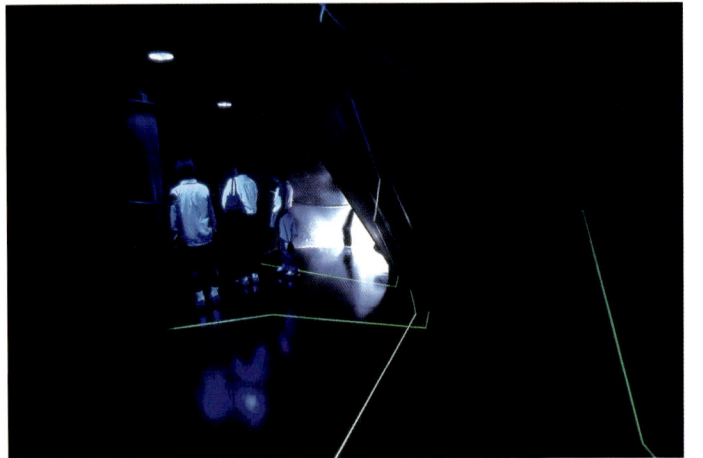 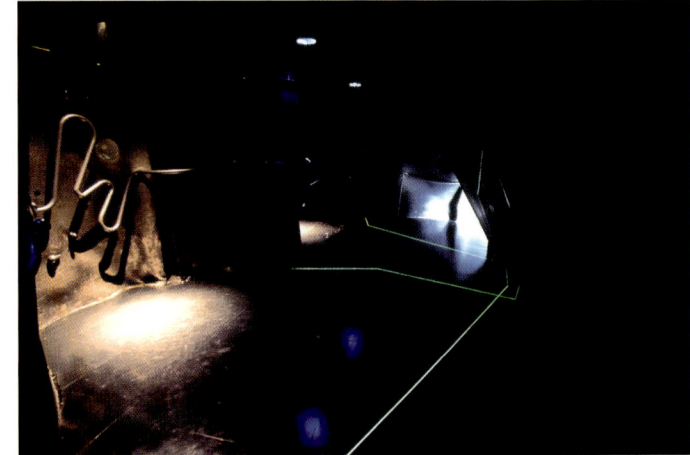

身体感覚をとりもどすエリアから膜壁空間への接
天の路と呼んだ鏡の筒。万華鏡の中に入る
床壁も空と化す。無数の空色。雲太陽。
まぶしすぎて目が開かない光の海。
曇の日。雨の日。そして雪の日も来る。嵐の中では流れる雲は
どうだろう。
ブルマー・イリュジョン。浮遊の中で。
月光の夜は楽しめて。夕日の赤もいいかもしれない。
風の日は雲が飛んで動いてくれる
その時は巨大な世界が広がります。

AIR TORAVERSE

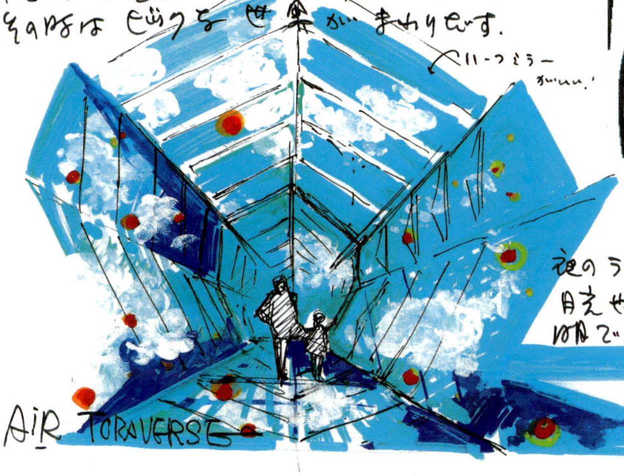

夏の陽ざしはきつい。ハーフミラーの反射＋井戸からの散水装置
をつける。水を流すとガラスの表面にわずかな水紋ができる。そのゆらめきは期待できる筈。
夜のライトアップは。光の筋が走るといい。流れ星のように。
月光や星との光で、歩行は可能と思えるが照明は最小限
の光でいい。

この路は登り。末広がりなので、何処から何えて
いくつあるのか？
10.oct. 六角鬼丈

瞑想空間のひとつか。放心、心を解き放てるか。心胡器セットと命名してプロジェクトをやったのは30年も昔になるタ谷典からのアロデュースのため。もっと郁まってコンサートで指揮。これでもかこれでもかと、視覚的にゆり籠をうしの人の自由性。優雅からゆり籠すのは演劇や映画の方がわかりやすい。ここでは黒塗の金に円8に入る8る8分

円、円筒、球は波が反響して、空間の圧がかかる。
隔円体、ラグビーボールが2つ組合さる。どんな音空間ができるのか。
音差、反響をもいしる室内楽器とちなる水滴がパラパラと落ちてくる水琴窟とこれも少し違うo。
ひと声、それ以上の心に響く、柔かい音の重なりが空間を包んでくれたらば。空間の匂がかってもよい。
α波の生なら……

で入る。ぶつかってもらえればよい。半覚半酔の中で、イメージの中で心を映しだす映画や、記憶の連鎖の中で……

白い双子官。左右ピンハート形にも見えて、心臓そのもの。

心胡器の仕様は2つの隔円体のつぎ目の形、ディテールは!

小さなホールで沈で全体自遠内外カバー。

AC リクエスト。
香りの装置(テーベナ)に付加。

金は反射、遠咽ながら映出

Lighting Program Fade in to Fade out   sound

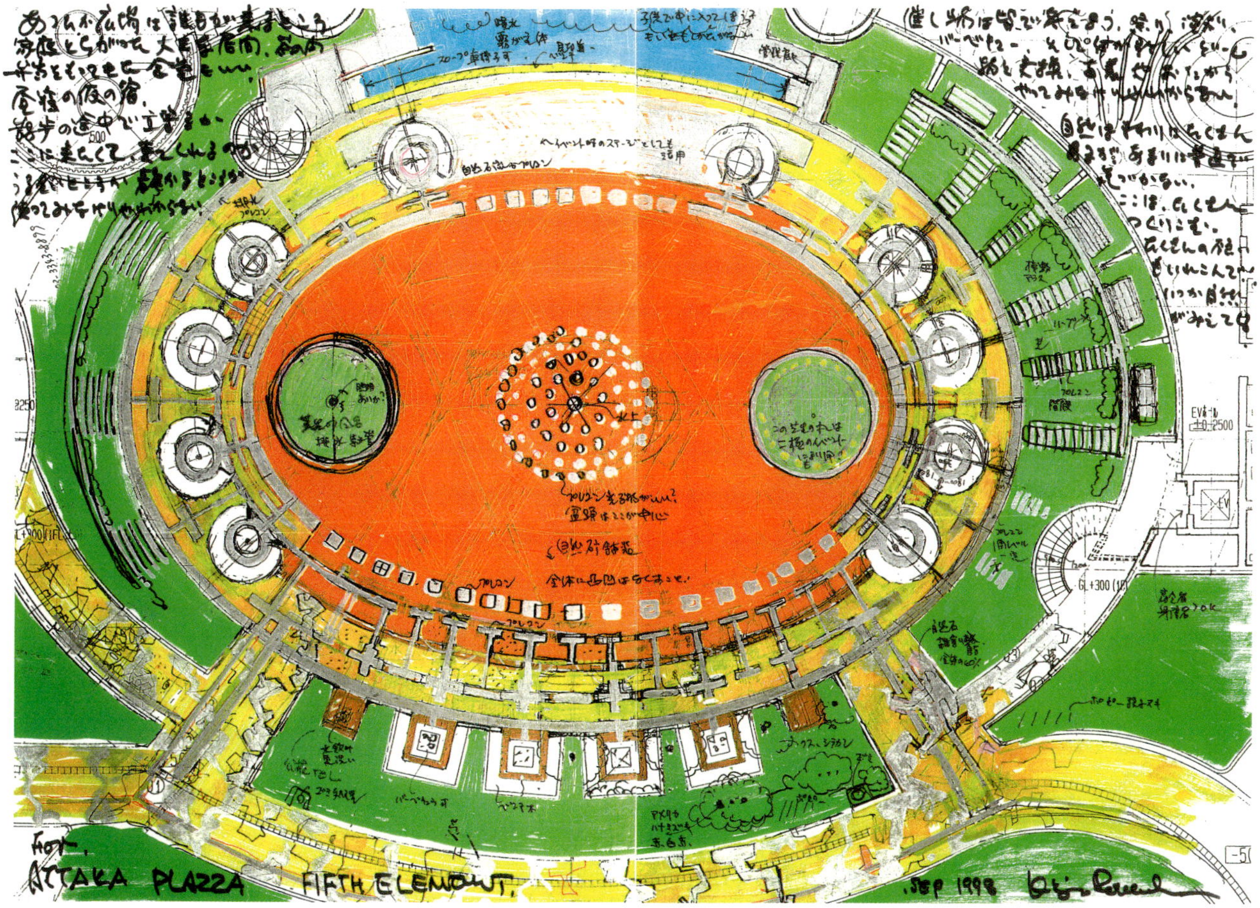
ATTAKA PLAZZA
FIFTH ELEMENT
SEP 1998

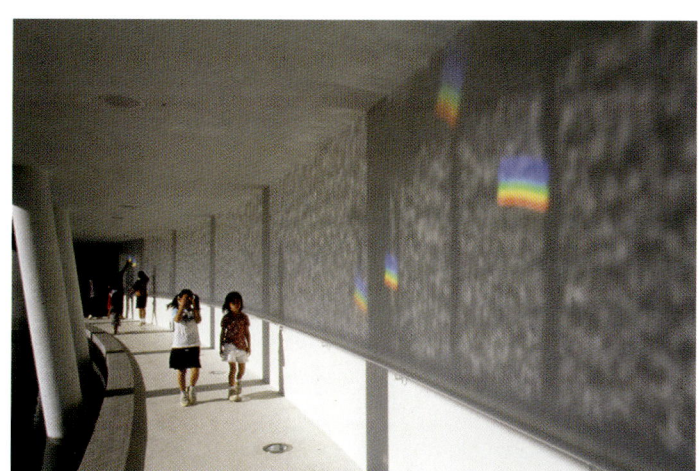

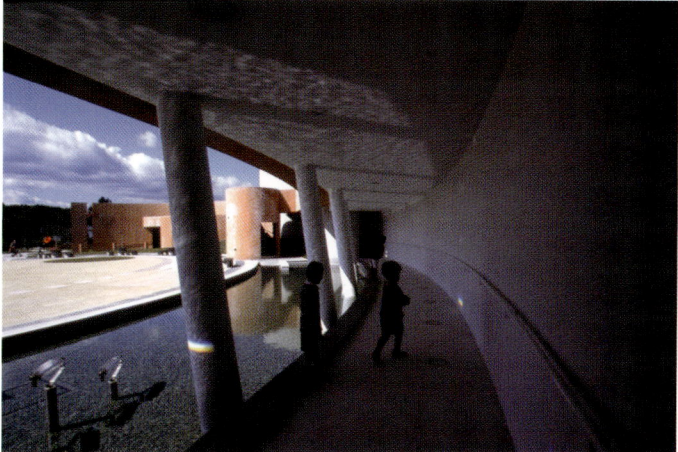

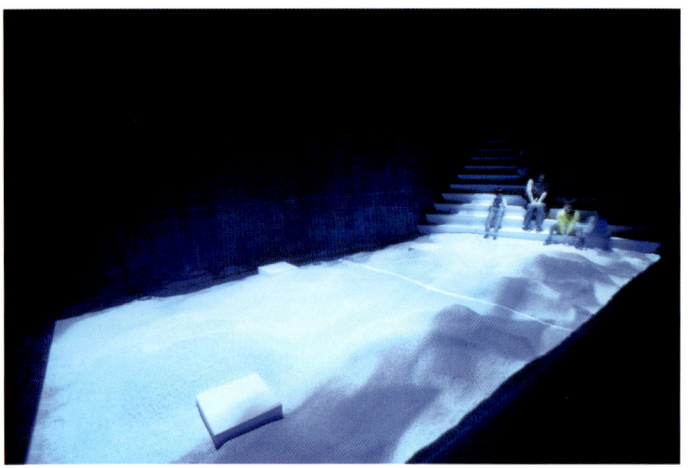

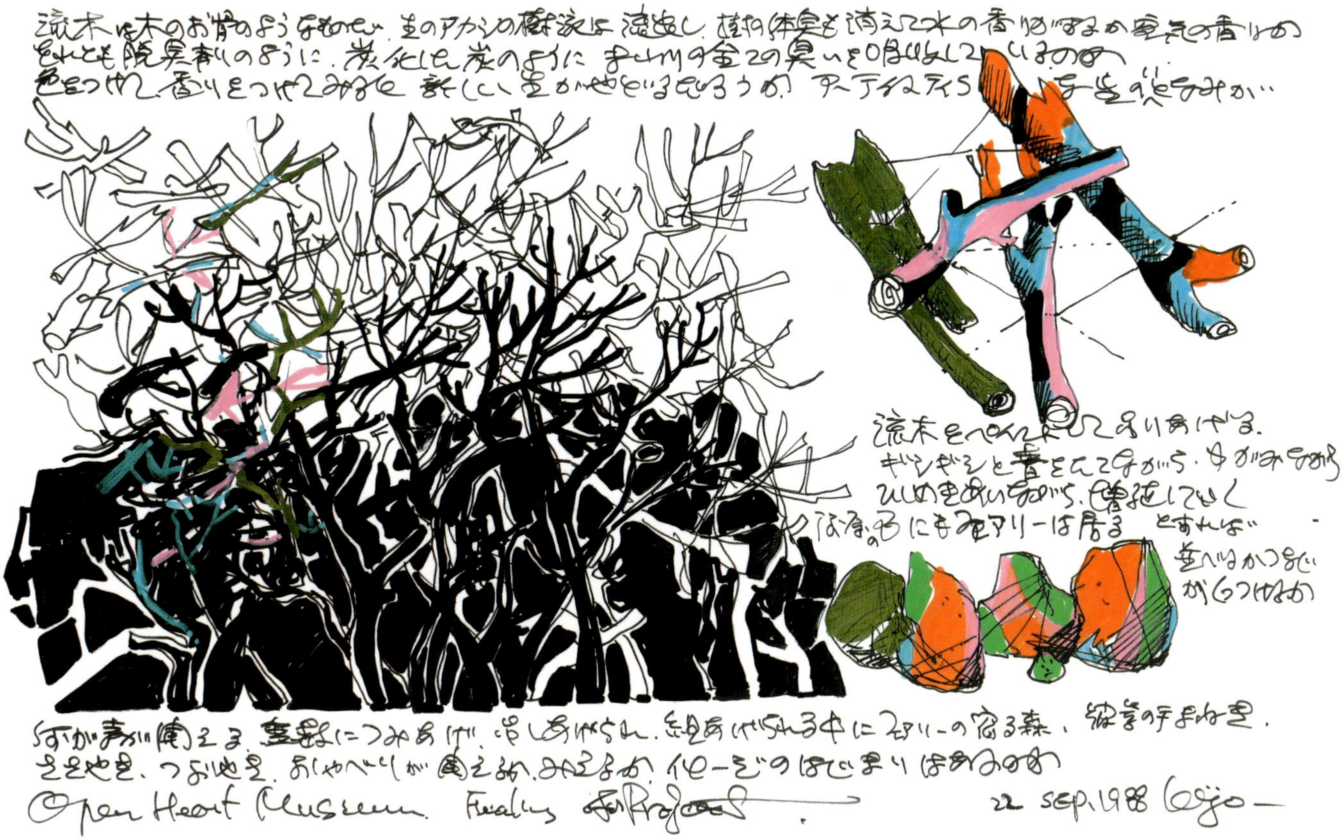

流木は木のお骨のようで恐い。生のアカシの腐敗臭に混迷し超物体臭を消えて水の香りがするか空気の香りかあれとも腐臭臭いのか。炭化した炭の上にまがりて金その臭いを吸収しているものに色つけて香りをつけてみたら新しい生命を得るだろうか。アフォダィス／子生のとたみか…

流木をへんしんさせてつりあげる。
ギシギシと音をたてながら。女が立ちあがる
ひめきあいながら、階段していく
石の下にも石の中にもマリーは居る とすれば
並べるかつむるか
かくつけるか

すがた声が聞こえる。霊気につみあがげる・消しあげられる・組みあげられる中にマリーの宿る森。終章の手よぬき要。
そそ地点。つぶ地点。おしゃべりが聞こえる。みえるかイメージのはじまりはあるのか
Open Heart Museum. Finaling ⚭Project○○   22 Sep. 1988 Ojo—

目の前に広がる風景の中に 風や水や木々の声が聞こえる。
集中心が高まると、もっと繊細に、そして大きく聞こえはじめ
体の中を流れる血液や心臓の鼓動と重なり、暑く涼しく
音から体温に移りてる。
鳥の声、虫の声、だんだん吹、役をまく人の足音や筆のきしみ
心地良き音から、車や街の生活音、ノイズなんとなく
気になる。
目から音の風景へ
と変化していく
人の感覚
目から耳へ
耳から目へ
脳の中で
何度も繰り返している感じは
本人にはわからない
で時々気合がかして
寄ってくる。その残響や
感度のゆらが
その場を動かしているらわかってくる。

Sound Scape と Ear's Project

本当は人がオブジェに掴みついていくのだが、
いかにもオブジェが掴まっていくようにつくる
オブジェの自然な形をするうねリズムとバランス。
人の寸法は気ずまるのだが、遊具としての
出入する動きを考えれば、ナガゆとリが出れば、
体をひねリ、大小うまく入リこめるのではないか。

混んだ電車、皆、力んで
いるとせまくてつかれる ね
ばらくすると力がぬけ
金体がゆれても気にする
痛せや、つっぱりは
体を大きくしてほう
らしい、もうまって
力をぬいて、
リラックス。
何か聞ったことの
ない音や声が聞こえる
脳の中に! 夢の中に!

10 oct 1998 Keiji Rokuden

71

Gateway Science School Courtyard

EDAW

St. Louis, Missouri, USA   photographs: contributed by EDAW

The outdoor environment at Gateway Science School allows students to investigate the 600-million-year history of life on Earth, play inside a model of the Pythagorean Theorem, manipulate a 70-foot-long water flume, and learn about the role of fire in nature by watching the actual burning of a prairie. To create a clear sense of organization in the two-acre open space, the courtyard is divided into two sections, with math and science elements grouped at the western end and natural science elements toward the east.

The math and science playground helps students grasp abstract concepts by providing physical examples. For instance, the sandbox has the shape of a right triangle surrounded by grid markings along the sides, graphically illustrating the Pythagorean Theorem. Other areas divided into grids of different sizes can be used for math games and puzzles. Two-foot cubes with numbers and math symbols printed on them can serve equally well as building blocks for forts or equations. Three six-foot-high cones double as play structures for crawling through and models of geometric properties. As a result, students have a chance to physically experience the concepts of volumes and planes.

To help students develop an ability to convert to the metric system, the main path leading to the playground takes the form of a large-scale measuring stick, a 50-meter-long yellow stripe with measurements marked in meters on one side and yards on the other.

The physics area includes a functional windmill and weather station, an area for students to experiment with levers, and a hydraulics lab. The hydraulics lab includes a 70-foot-long spiral flume water workshop. Workstations at different heights allow students to manipulate water in the flume, create dams and locks, study erosion, and observe how different configurations alter water flow and water pressure.

The math-science area features a scale model of the full solar system on the ground plane, correctly showing the spatial relationships of the planets and the sun. Ten-foot-wide bands of colored concrete mark off distances of 400 million kilometers. Bronze medallions indicate the location of planets in their orbits.

The stream provides students with opportunities to observe different kinds of aquatic life as it crosses over rocky outcroppings and splashes down a cascade to a pond. A bluff near the stream was fashioned of Missouri limestone, the predominant sedimentary rock in the state. Here, children can hunt for fossils embedded in the limestone and take rubbings.

To connect students interactively with the history of life on Earth, the courtyard includes a Time Walk that crosses a bridge to the wetlands area. Each 17-foot-long segment chronicles 50 million years with visual and tactile components.

The prairie shows students what much of the area was like before modern civilization changed the landscape. Native grasses and wildflowers, as well as birdhouses, attract a wide variety of insect and bird life. Students participate in collecting seeds and propagating plants. Once a year, everyone gathers in the amphitheater to watch the burning of the prairie, which dramatically illustrates the natural life cycle of prairies. The wetlands serve as a safety buffer between students and the fire.

Students can enter the wetlands area via a wooden boardwalk. The wetlands surround the pond, stocked with fish, frogs, turtles, and waterfowl, where students engage in hands-on learning activities such as collecting tadpoles.

The courtyard also features four 1,000-square-foot cloisters, which are fenced-in areas each assigned exclusively to a particular set of grade levels. All cloisters contain raised planting beds. Assigning students their own area to plant and tend encourages them to think of themselves as stewards of their environment.

Throughout, EDAW took care to design the courtyard not as a science museum full of signs interpreting concepts for students, but rather an artistically composed unified landscape that subtly encourages interactive learning, questioning and dialog.

75

The Quarries
Taylor Cullity Lethlean & Mary Jeavons

Clifton Hill, Victoria, Australia photographs: Taylor Cullity Lethlean

The Quarries is a regional play space which utilises quarry and industrial images from the site's past to create elevated decks and bridges among constructed cliff faces, caves and tunnels.

The project involved consultation with local residents and sporting clubs to develop active and passive recreational spaces with particular emphasis on the design of a wide variety of play opportunities for children. Our approach was to maximise play opportunities while using quality and crafted materials that stimulate children's imagination and challenge them physically. Vandalism, maintenance considerations, disabled access and knowledge of safety standards all played an important part in our design process. The design was conceived as a labyrinth created from the repetition of vertical poles, painted in a vibrant and engaging colour. The poles form an oversized forest, partially sunken beneath the adjacent levels, and the armature for containing detailed play elements for senior and junior play. The formal arrangement creates a sculptural field through which children can chase, hide and explore. Corridors are defined connecting entry points to the play elements. In association with the vibrant red structure, soft surfaces of pea gravel and adjacent rolling lawns create further play opportunities.

This is a place of fun, of hide and seek, a chance to get lost, spy, discover and imagine.

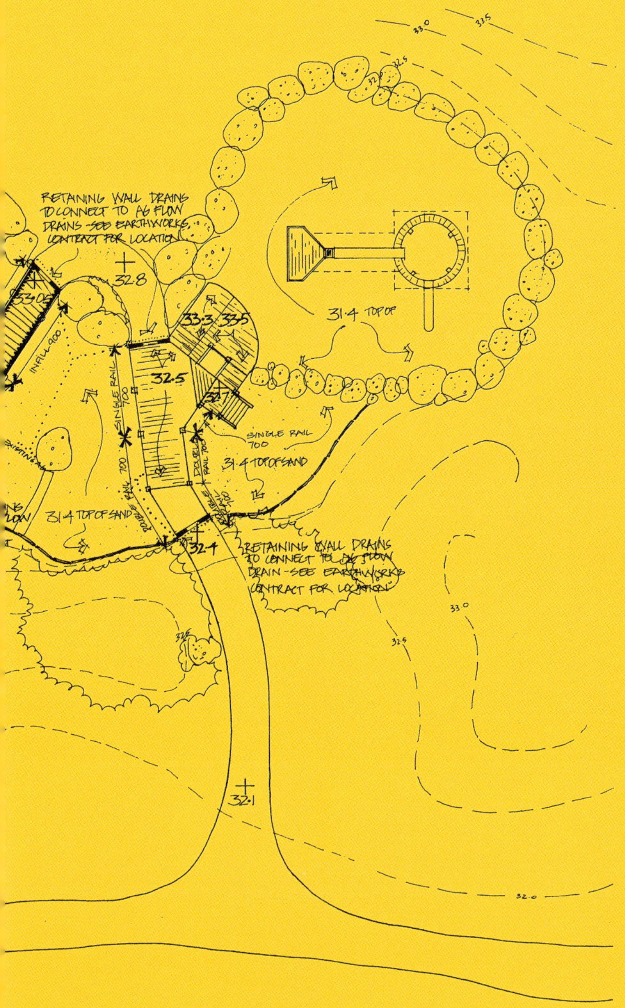
RETAINING WALL DRAINS TO CONNECT TO AG FLOW DRAINS-SEE EARTHWORKS CONTRACT FOR LOCATION
32.8
33.3-33.5
31.4 TOP OF
32.5
SINGLE RAIL 700
31.4 TOP OF SAND
31.4 TOP OF SAND
RETAINING WALL DRAINS TO CONNECT TO AG FLOW DRAIN-SEE EARTHWORKS CONTRACT FOR LOCATION
32.1

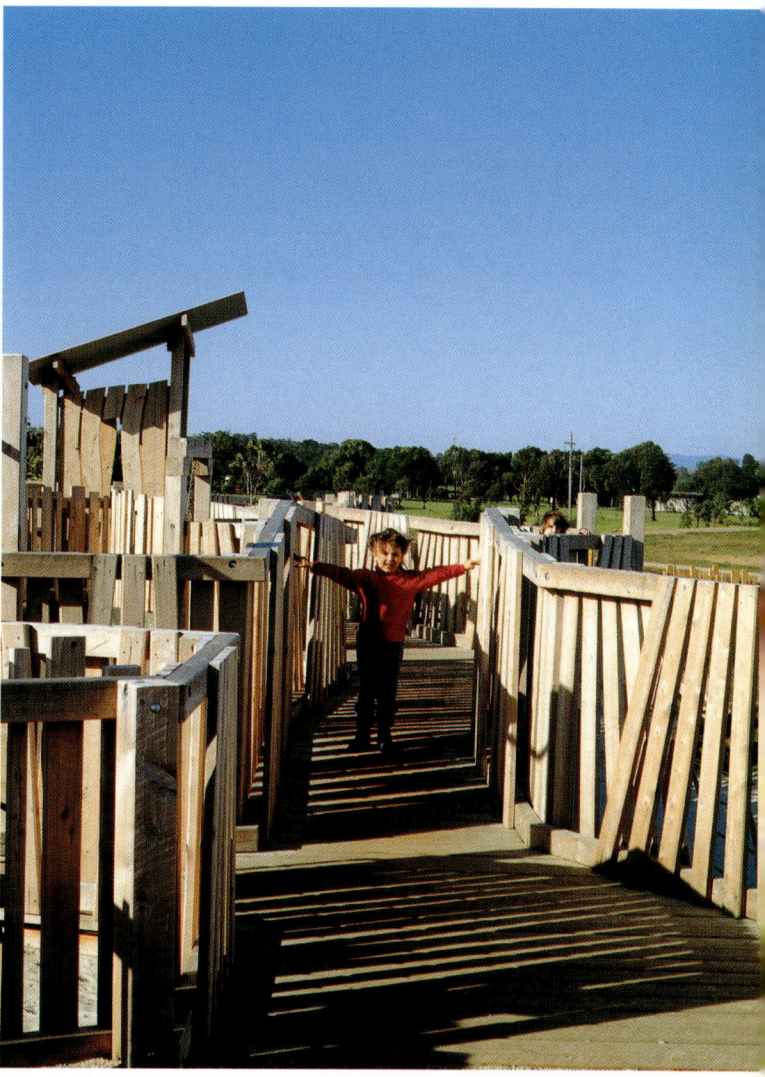

80

Hamamatsu Science Museum

Mitsuru Senda + Environment Design Institute

Hamamatsu City, Shizuoka, Japan

photographs: Mitsumasa Fujitsuka

This museum was planned on a one-hectare site set adjacent to the Shinkansen (bullet train) line as part of the redevelopment of the south exit area of Hamamatsu Station. With a total floor area of nearly 7000 square meters, the museum has four above-ground floors and a partial steel structure.

The concept for the museum was to communicate to children the venturesome scientific spirit of world-class Hamamatsu-based companies, such as Honda, Yamaha, Suzuki, and Kawai, thereby transmitting the idea that science can be exciting, as well as bring about palpable results and benefits.

Planned clearly as an Exploratorium and circular play system, the architectural concept was that of a scientific exhibit. The intention behind the predominant shapes and colors was to engage children's interest in order to bring them closer, to where the didactic aspect of each display unfolds in a much more fascinating and fun way than in their science textbooks.

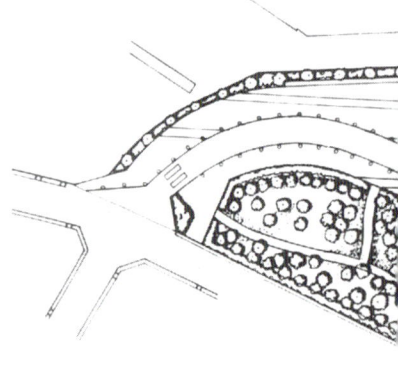

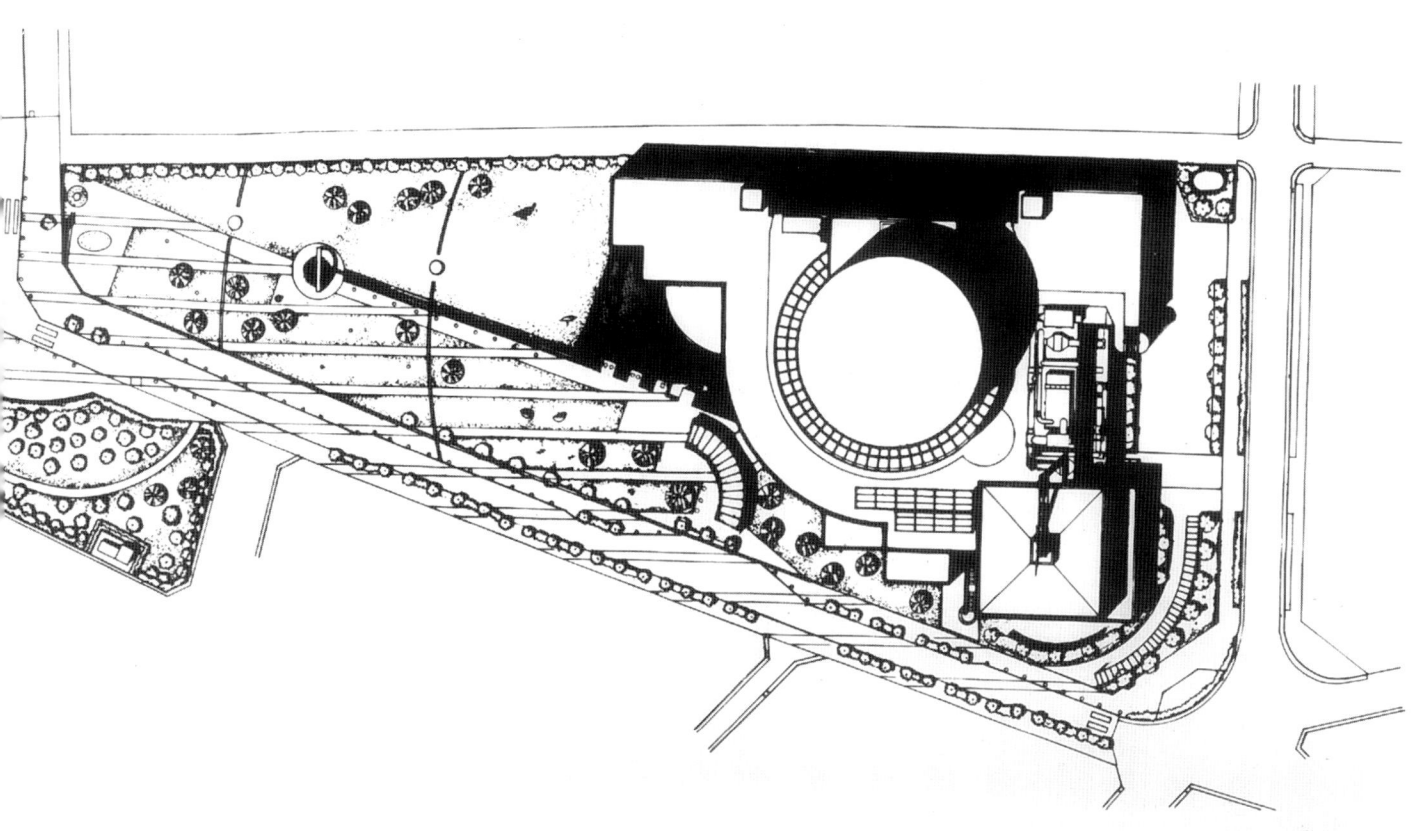

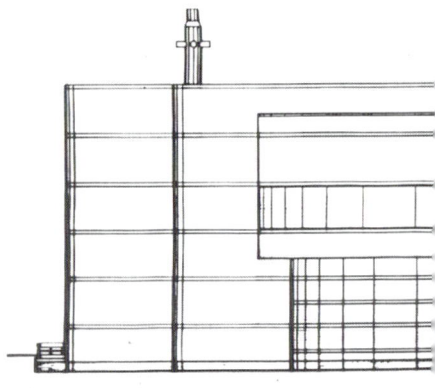

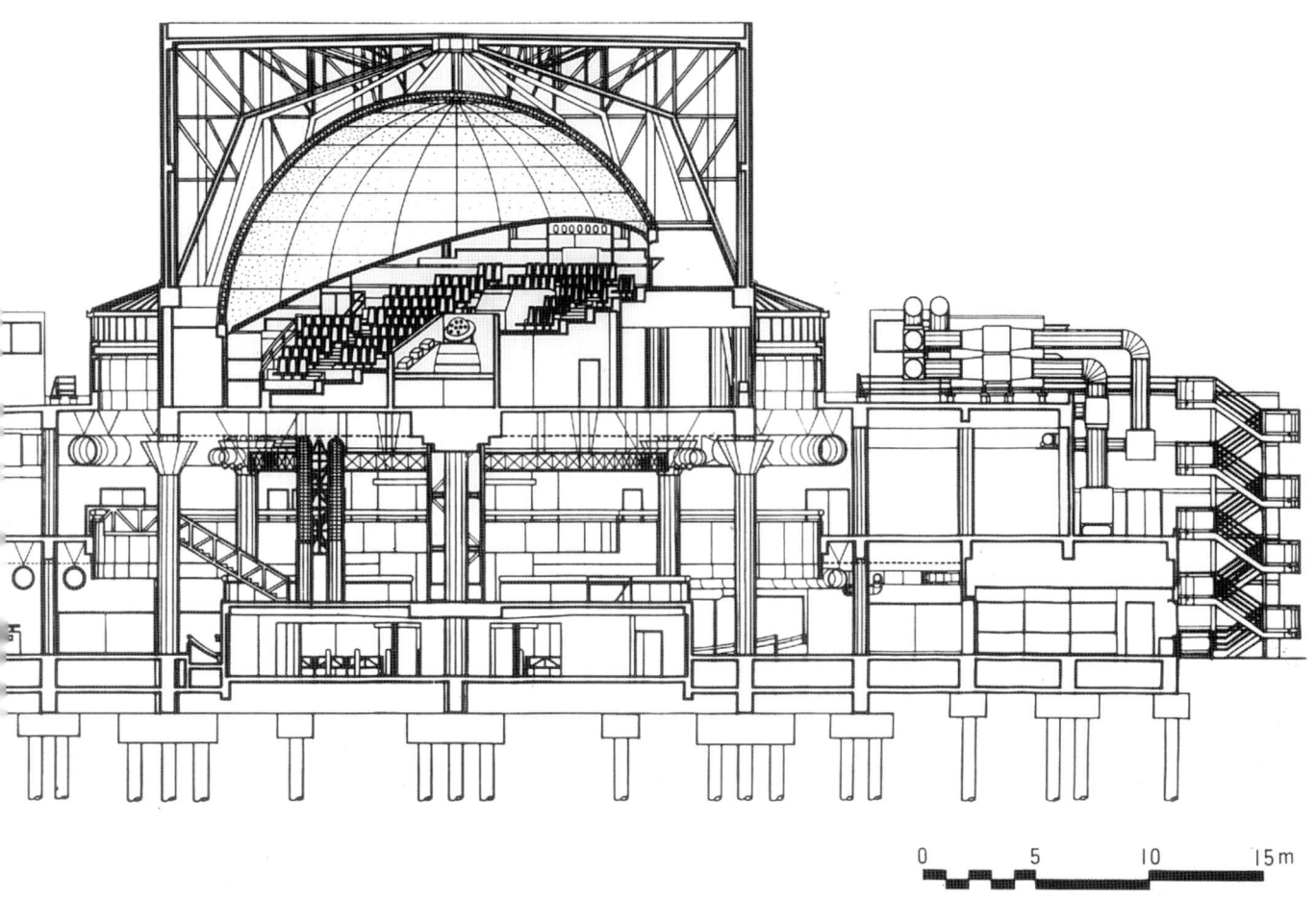

87

Parc Astérix

Isabelle Devin & Catherine Rannou

Plailly, France

photographs: Isabelle Devin

In the heart of the Astérix amusement park (which is based on the popular comic book character of the same name), located 50 kilometers outside of Paris, this play space has been set up in the park's original setting: the forest.

Intended for children of up to twelve years, this 4000-square-meter space provides visual and sensory stimuli that create a fantastical atmosphere set somewhere between reality and artifice. The pristine natural surroundings of the playground seem to automatically transport the children into another dimension in time.

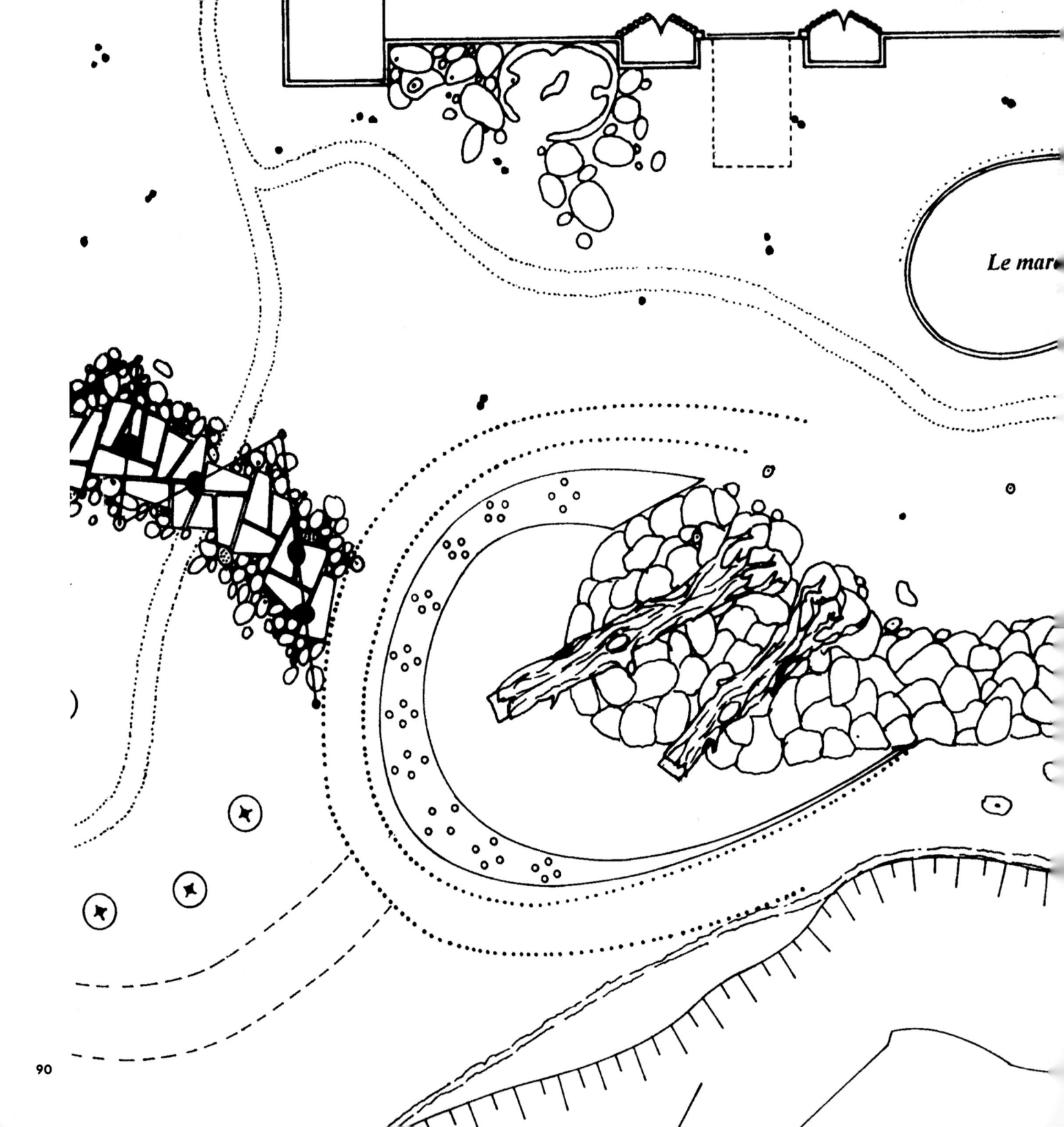

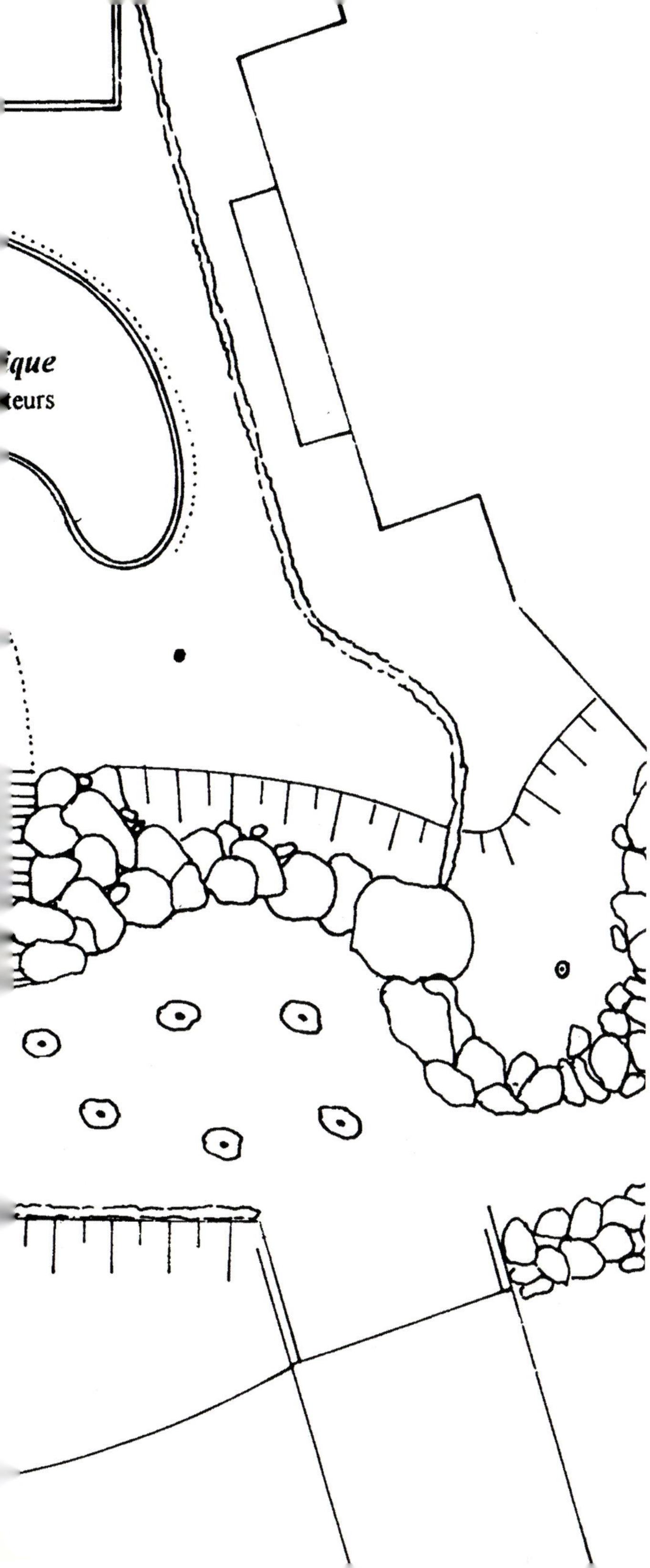

ique
teurs

© A. GUI

91

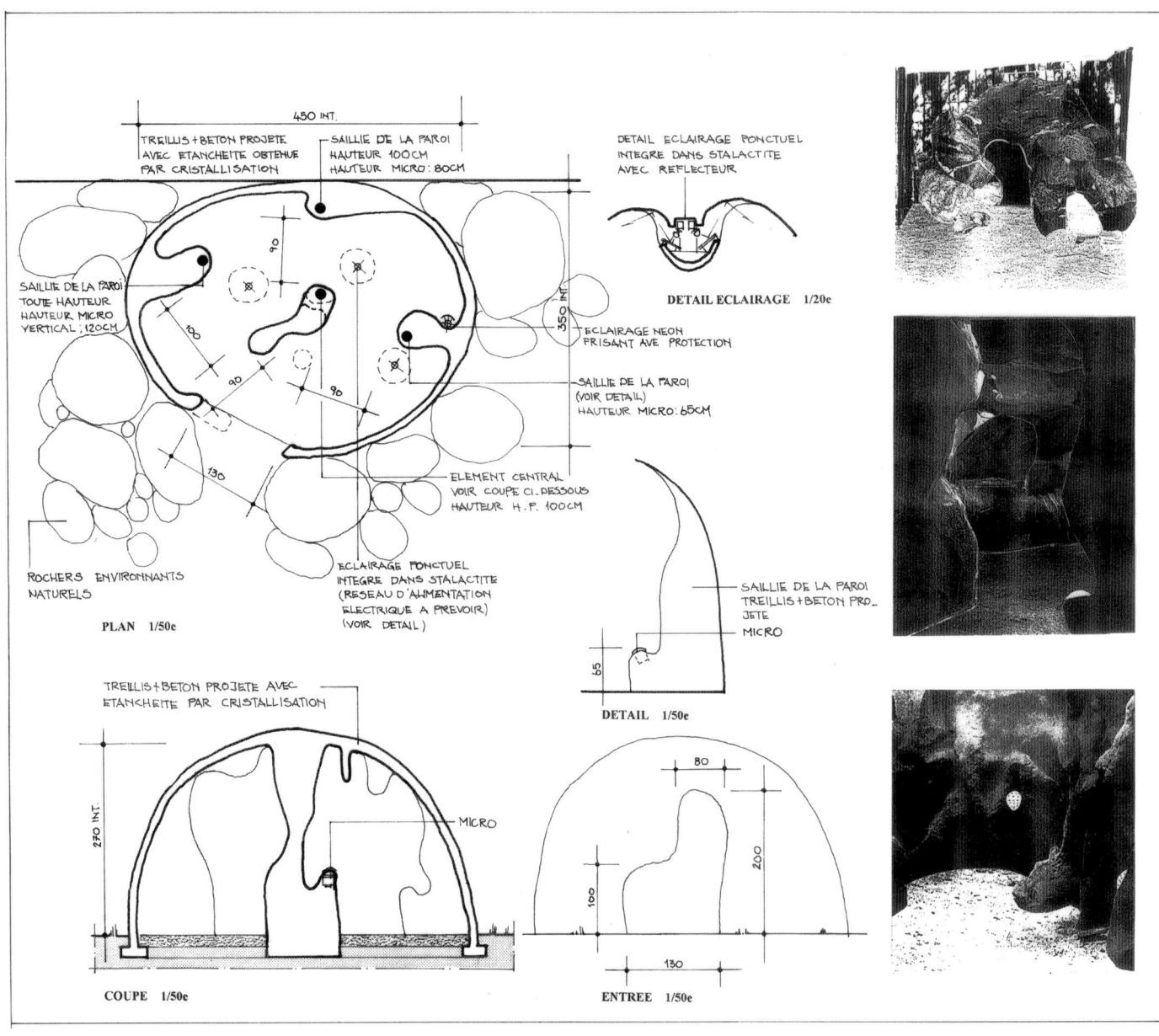

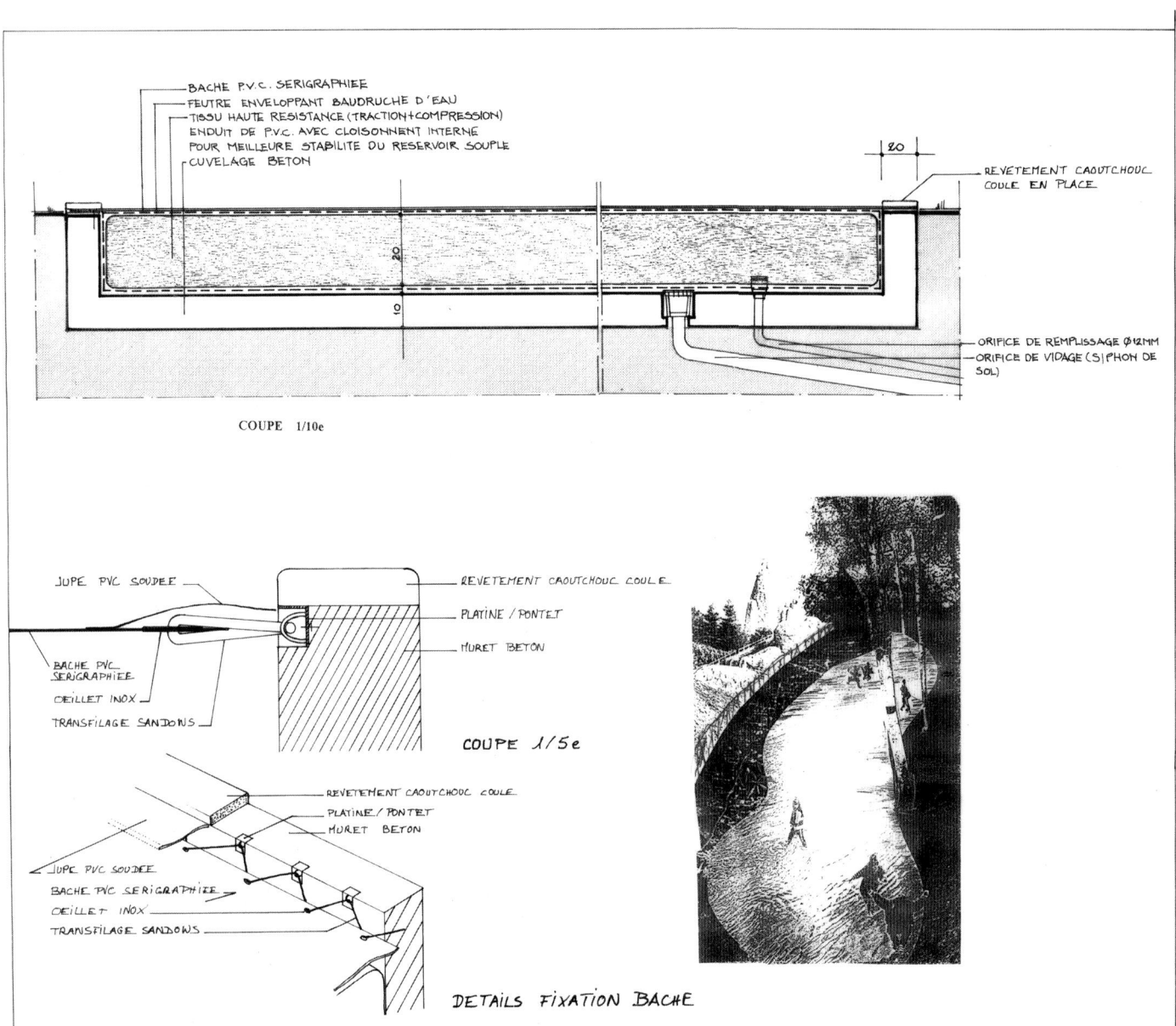

© A.GUI

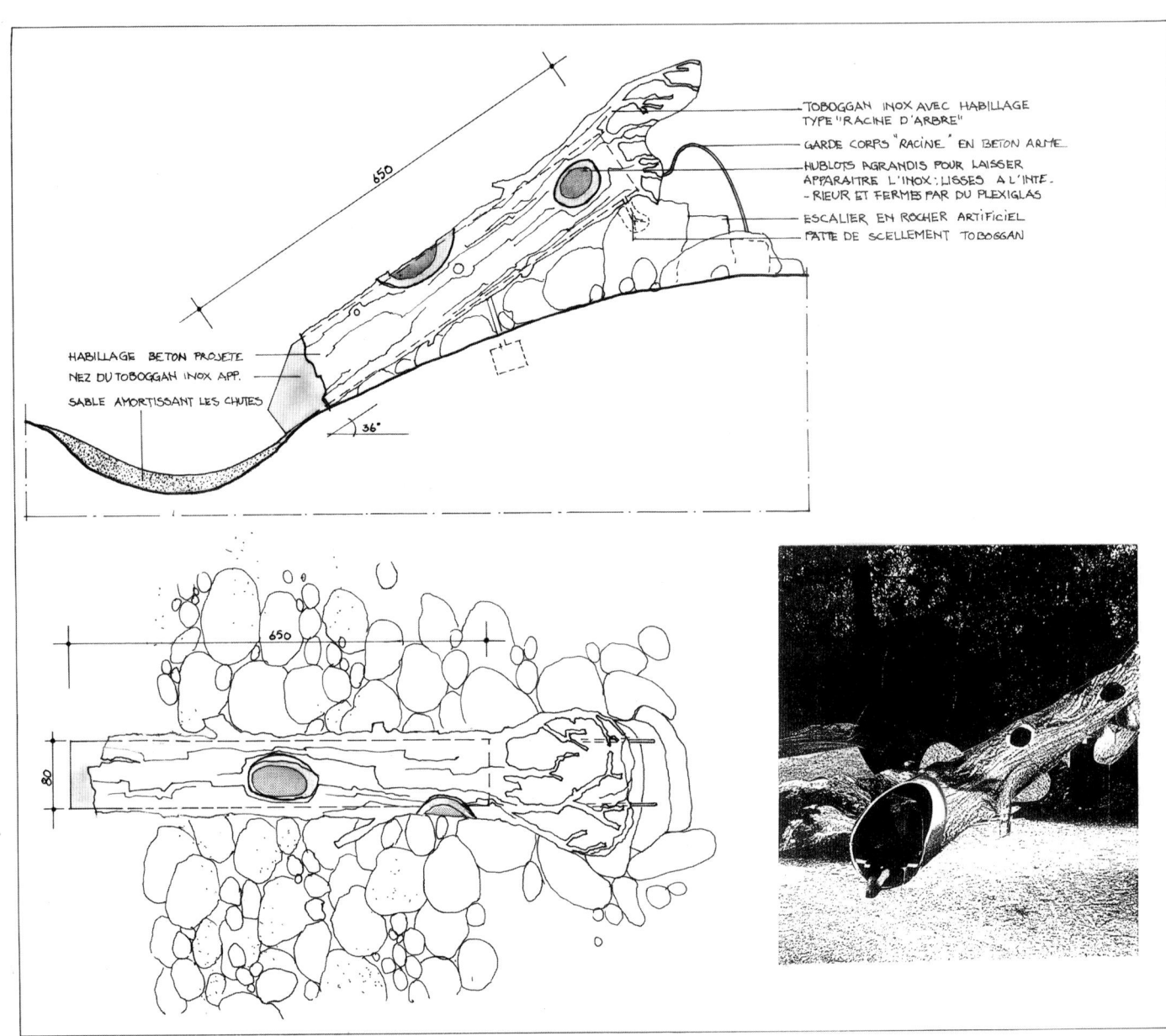

© A.GUI

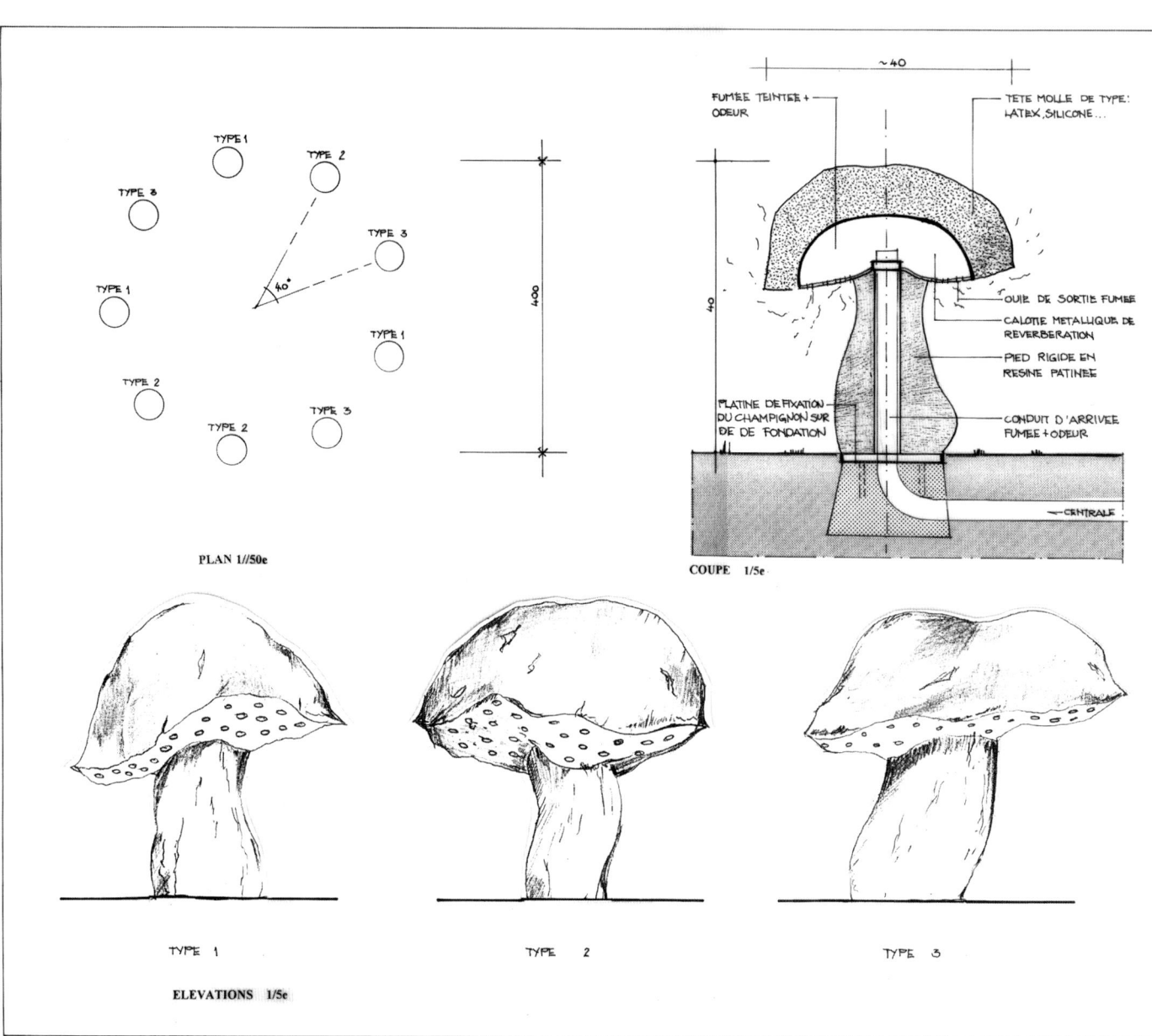

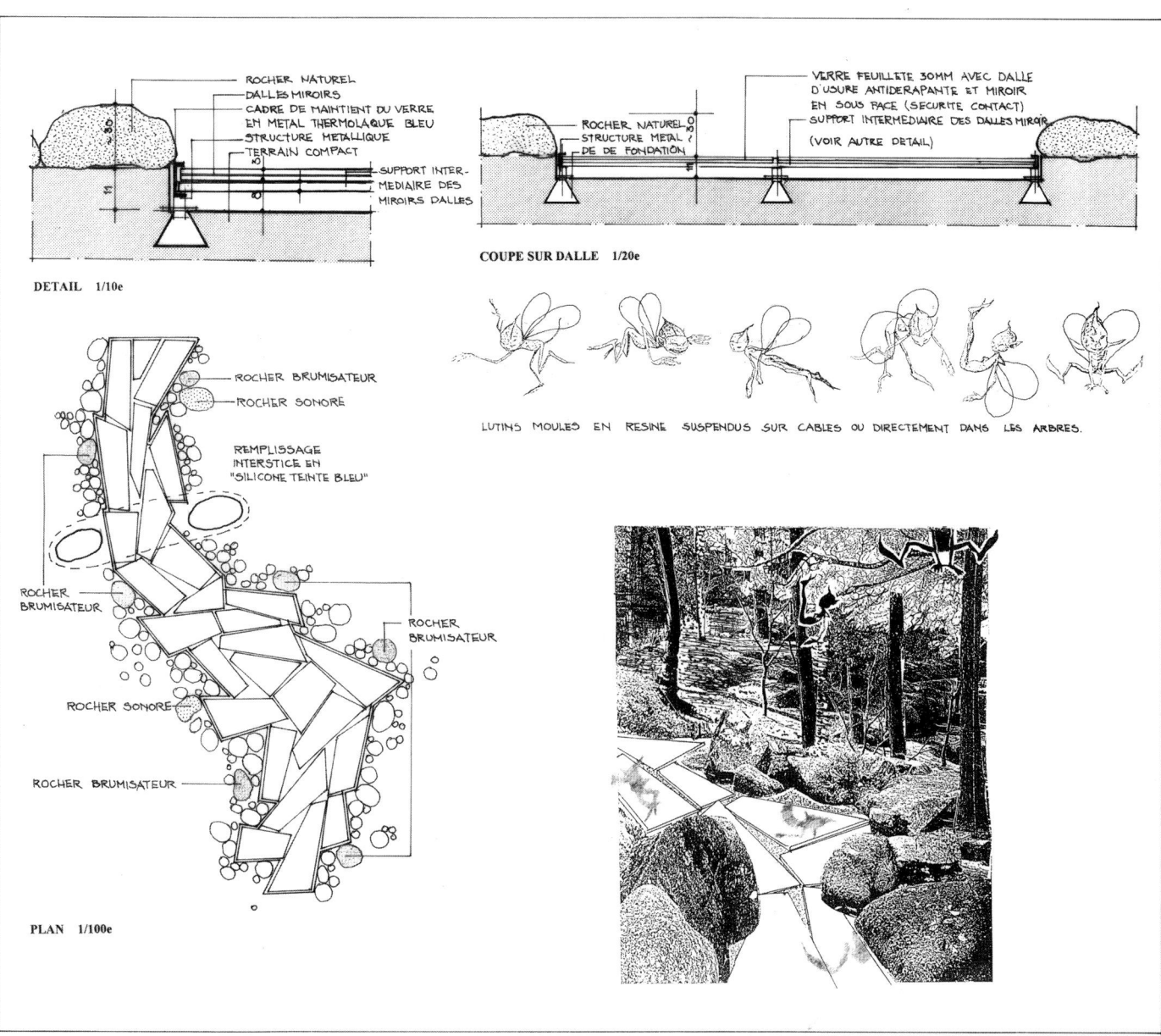

DETAIL 1/10e

- ROCHER NATUREL
- DALLES MIROIRS
- CADRE DE MAINTIEN DU VERRE EN METAL THERMOLAQUE BLEU
- STRUCTURE METALLIQUE
- TERRAIN COMPACT
- SUPPORT INTERMEDIAIRE DES MIROIRS DALLES

COUPE SUR DALLE 1/20e

- ROCHER NATUREL
- STRUCTURE METAL DE DE FONDATION
- VERRE FEUILLETE 30MM AVEC DALLE D'USURE ANTIDERAPANTE ET MIROIR EN SOUS FACE (SECURITE CONTACT)
- SUPPORT INTERMEDIAIRE DES DALLES MIROIR (VOIR AUTRE DETAIL)

LUTINS MOULES EN RESINE SUSPENDUS SUR CABLES OU DIRECTEMENT DANS LES ARBRES.

PLAN 1/100e

- ROCHER BRUMISATEUR
- ROCHER SONORE
- REMPLISSAGE INTERSTICE EN "SILICONE TEINTE BLEU"
- ROCHER BRUMISATEUR
- ROCHER BRUMISATEUR
- ROCHER SONORE
- ROCHER BRUMISATEUR

Ross's Landing Park and Plaza

EDAW

Chattanooga, Tennessee, USA

photographs: Contributed by EDAW

Around 1815 John Ross established a riverside trading settlement here; yet the Industrial Revolution filled the area in with factories and warehouses, separating the city from the river. Finally, in the 1980s, the area became the focus of a major urban redevelopment effort. A new $45 million aquarium project provided an opportunity for a new plaza and park that connects the river to the city once again. Completed in 1992, Ross's Landing enhances the aquarium's educational mission, creatively employing architecture, artifacts, and native plantings to tell the story of the region's cultural and natural history.

To dramatically integrate city and nature, past and present, 35 alternating bands of hardscape and landscape trace Chattanooga's history and ecology. One of the bands rises into the air to form a ceremonial entry arch, which echoes the form of the mountains beyond with softly curving shapes. Nearby, a fountain also mimics the mountain profiles with its rows of water jets.

As visitors pass through the entry arch and approach the river, they are also moving back through time. Historic artifacts scattered throughout each band chronicle a different era in local history. For example, Chattanooga once hosted the original Coca-Cola bottling plant. To commemorate this, pieces of Coca-Cola bottles are embedded in one of the concrete bands, and a bridge set with bottle bottoms crosses the stream. In another area, pavers in the form of railroad tracks pay a tribute to the region's railroading history with the song lyrics for "Chattanooga Choo Choo". In the children's play area, cannon balls, musket pieces, uniform buckles and other Civil War memorabilia are embedded in stones stacked to recall the natural limestone bluffs of the region. Other areas feature castings of Native American pottery, a memorial to blues singer Bessie Smith, pavers with a design inspired by Appalachian quilts, and pavers that tell tribal Cherokee myths illustrated with sculpted animals.

In the late 1830s, the US Army forced thousands of Cherokees to march through Tennessee from ancestral homelands to Oklahoma: the Trail of Tears. Thousands of Cherokees died along the way. In memory, the chronology of events is engraved on a series of pavement tiles, some of which have cracks symbolizing the broken promises to the Native Americans. Four thousand white crocuses planted in the same landscape band, along with Cherokee Princess and Chieftain dogwood trees, serve as a living memory to those who perished.

Ross's Landing was designed with children of all ages in mind. To entertain children visiting the park or waiting to enter the aquarium, a stream course runs throughout the site. A variety of pools, rapids, and falls mimic the area's natural water flows and provide an ever-changing experience. Kids can follow the water and discover the park's different aspects. Pre-cast concrete replicas of native alligator gar fish lurk in the stream bottom -- children find these quickly and play with them. In addition, they can hop from one steppingstone to another through the stream. Taking into account different age groups, some of the water features are tame and shallow, while others are knee-deep and encourage more activity.

A series of terrace seat-walls invite running, jumping, and hide-and-seek games. The seats also feature cast animal sculptures. Throughout, multiple seating and shaded areas on the edges of play environments allow parents opportunities for quiet observation.

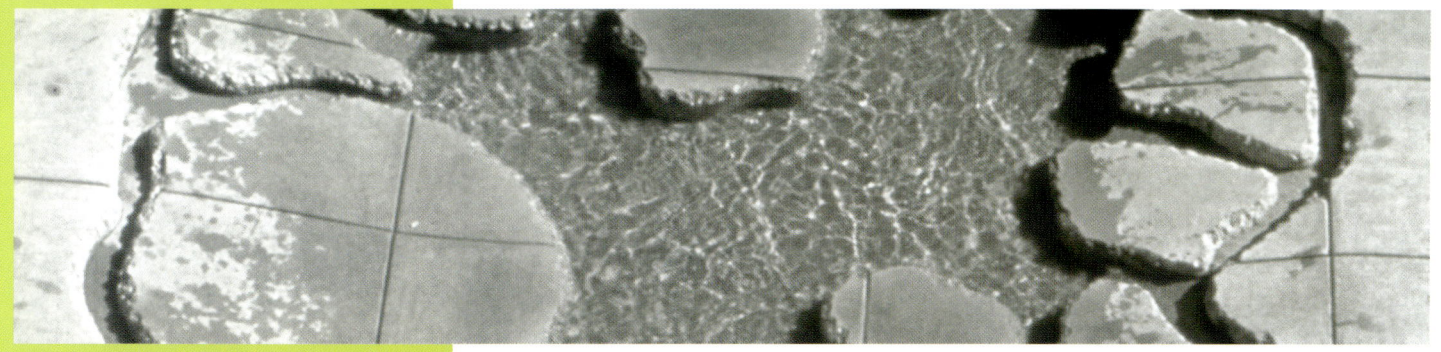

103

Murergaarden

Helle Nebelong

Norrebro, Copenhagen, Denmark

photographs: Helle Nebelong

The age of the 164 children at the school ranges from one to fourteen and the total play area is limited to barely 1050 square meters that had previously been split into two separate playgrounds with a fence dividing them. There was also an existing difference in level of some 2 meters - a difference which became a focal point of the design.

With the old 1970s playground in derelict condition, in 1996 the local authorities decided to hold a theme day on playgrounds for school officials. The employees of the institutions were asked to put forward their ideas on what would constitute the "perfect" playground. It was stressed right from the start that economic speculation should not come into play, but rather that it would be imagination alone, supported by pedagogical arguments, which would decide the final suggestion for a playground.

Although the planning process was carried out by adults, their ideas for the perfect playground came from listening to the children's preferences for the play area. The numerous suggestions were then compiled and the design for a new playground for Murergaarden was drawn up.

The result was a small, organically-shaped oasis, which sat in counterpoint to the massive surfaces of the surrounding buildings. The largest area of the playground is for the use of all the children, but it is possible to close off a smaller area for the toddlers. Although traditional play equipment was not on their list, they got a slide anyway!

The differing levels have been connected via a terraced slope, which has become a central feature in the playground. The little Tarmac-lined paddling pool is connected to a channel and spring on the upper part of the playground. In the summer a fire-hose is used to fill the steps with water, which flows down to the paddling pool. When filled, the water is turned off and the pool is emptied in the evening. The pool is encircled by willows, butterfly bushes and perennial flowers, which attract butterflies and other insects.

In spite of initial reservations that the space was dangerous or even boring, the children love the space and none have been seriously hurt in the five years of its existence. The parents now say that their children are happier when they come home; and the school principal says that there are fewer conflicts in the playground. Everyone is satisfied with the results of the playground, and particularly with the presence of water in it.

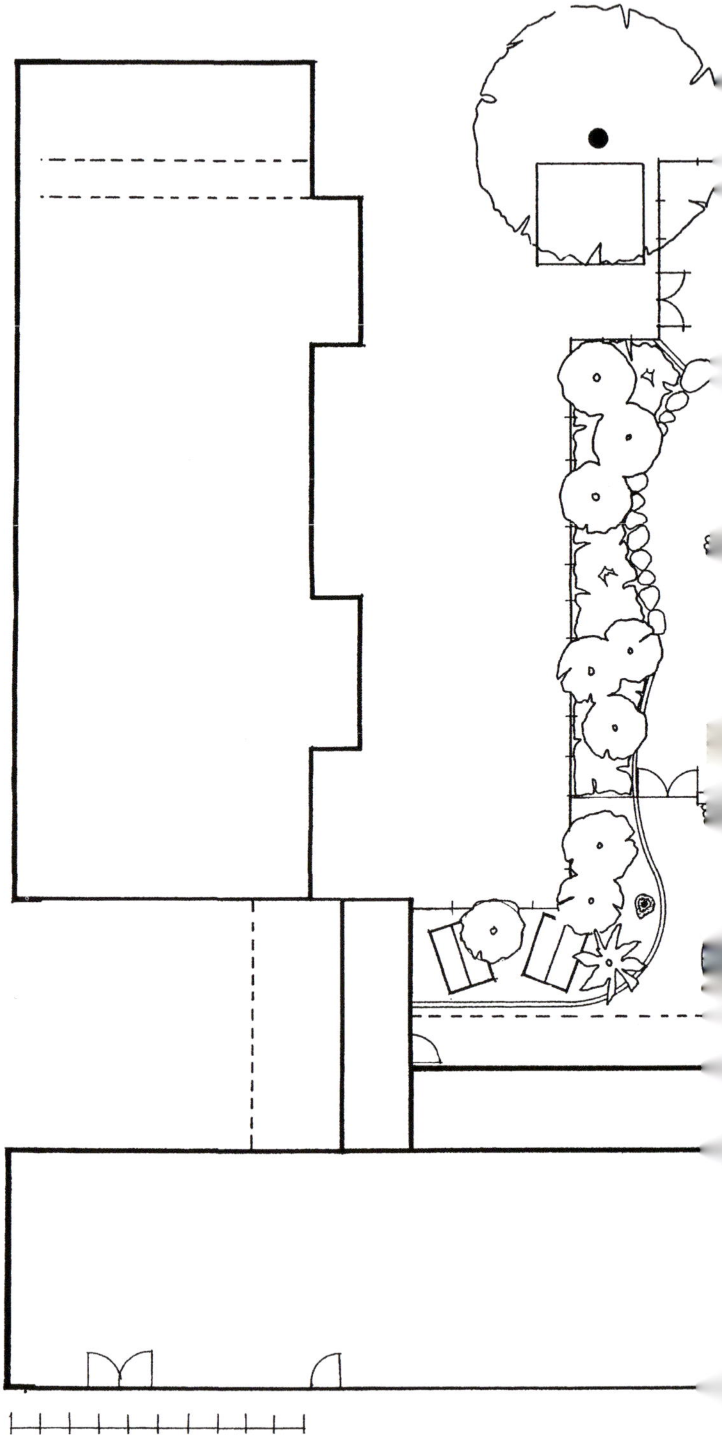

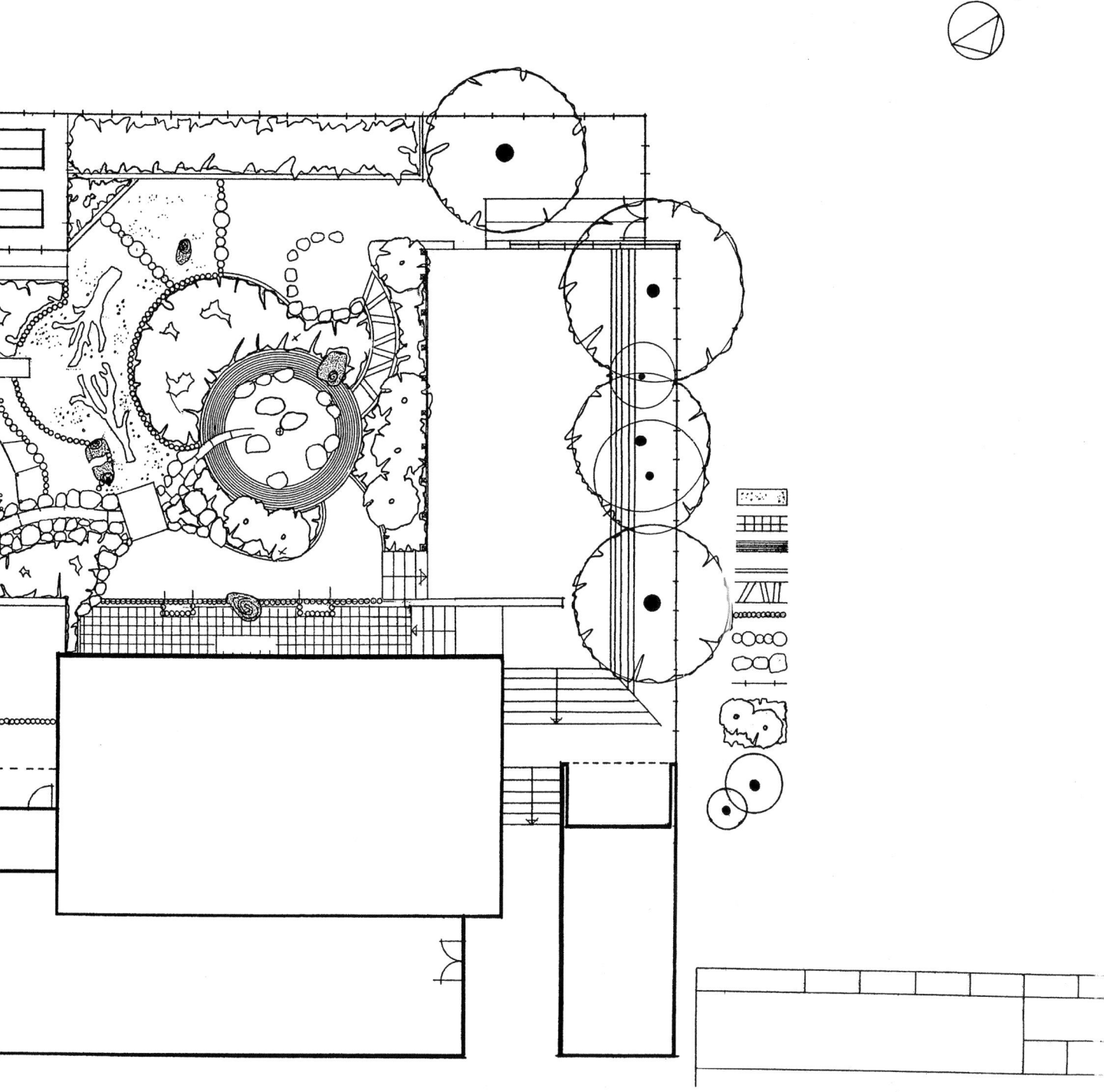

Tochigi Wanpaku Park

PREC Institute Inc.

Mibu, Tochigi Prefecture, Japan

photographs: Yohei Nagasaka & Hidefumi Tsuda

Comprising 37 hectares, the park is located in a rural area characterized by farmland and paddy fields. By conserving and enhancing the land's beautiful natural resources, large patches of vegetation and open fields were achieved where children have the space necessary to run and play.
The site's water was incorporated into the plan of the park and local tree species were cultivated, thereby creating a controlled biotope for a wide variety of organisms. This water-friendly aspect is especially attractive in Tochigi Prefecture, which is a landlocked region of the country.
As "Tochigi Children's Kingdom", Dream and Adventure were the themes of the park. The facilities were planned in such a way that the children are able to create their own games and let their imagination run free.

Plan

A. North gate plazza

B. Promenade

C. Flower Town
C-1 Kingdom Plaza
C-2 Flower of Dreams

D. Children's Village
D-1 Children's farm
D-2 Children's ranch

E. Breeze Valey
E-1 Breeze field
E-2 Flower garden
E-3 Muddy field

F. Wonder Forest
F-1 Wonder path
F-2 Fountain

G. Green Hill
G-1 Green maze
G-2 Adventure maze
G-3 Adventure lake
G-4 Adventure island
G-5 South gate plaza

H. Flower Castle

I. Children Market

J. Wonder Ship

K. Adventure Hut

L. Steam Engine Station

M. Parking Lot
M-1 North parking lot 1
M-2 North parking lot 2
M-3 South parking lot

SITE PLAN

Stepping Stones Museum for Children

Jefferson B. Riley, FAIA with Charles G. Mueller, AIA of Centerbrook
Centerbrook Architects and Planners

Norwalk, Connecticut, USA

photographs: Jeff Goldberg / ESTO

This museum was designed to encourage wonder and independent inquiry in children ages 1 to 10. Exhibits of science, culture, and local history are housed in two open shed wings that radiate out from the "Hub", the lobby of the museum. At the epicenter of the "Hub's" coiled shape is an interactive machine where children can advance balls of different sizes through a tower of augers, chutes, and trampolines. From the platform's heightened vantage point, all of the other offerings of the museum can be viewed. The two wings of the museum partially enclose an outdoor play space. A curving, trellised pergola completes the enclosure and provides a shaded sitting area for observers of kids at play.

The building works as an exhibit in and of itself. It not only exposes how ordinary things work, but also explores how they can work in unordinary ways. The tower becomes a person. Its windows are eyes, ears, and mouth, its nose a sundial. Its hat is also a birdcage in which flights of fancy are hatched. The hat is crowned with a "feathervane" in honor of the local folk hero, Yankee Doodle Dandy, who "stuck a feather in his hat and called it macaroni", as the song goes. There is even a macaroni path.

The air supply ducts in the Hub are arms of an octopus. Columns are trees. A stone wall becomes the tail of Tyrannosaurus Rex. Rain gutters turn into eyes of a smiling face that weeps when it rains. The Hub is a river filed with fish and stepping stones for children to hop along as they move through the museum. It is an extension of the stepping stone sidewalk outside. There is a hole in the floor where children can peer into the basement mechanical room. Pipes, ducts, wires, and structural connections are exposed throughout the rest of the building. The back of the theater opens like an airplane hangar to transform the outdoor playground into an amphitheater.

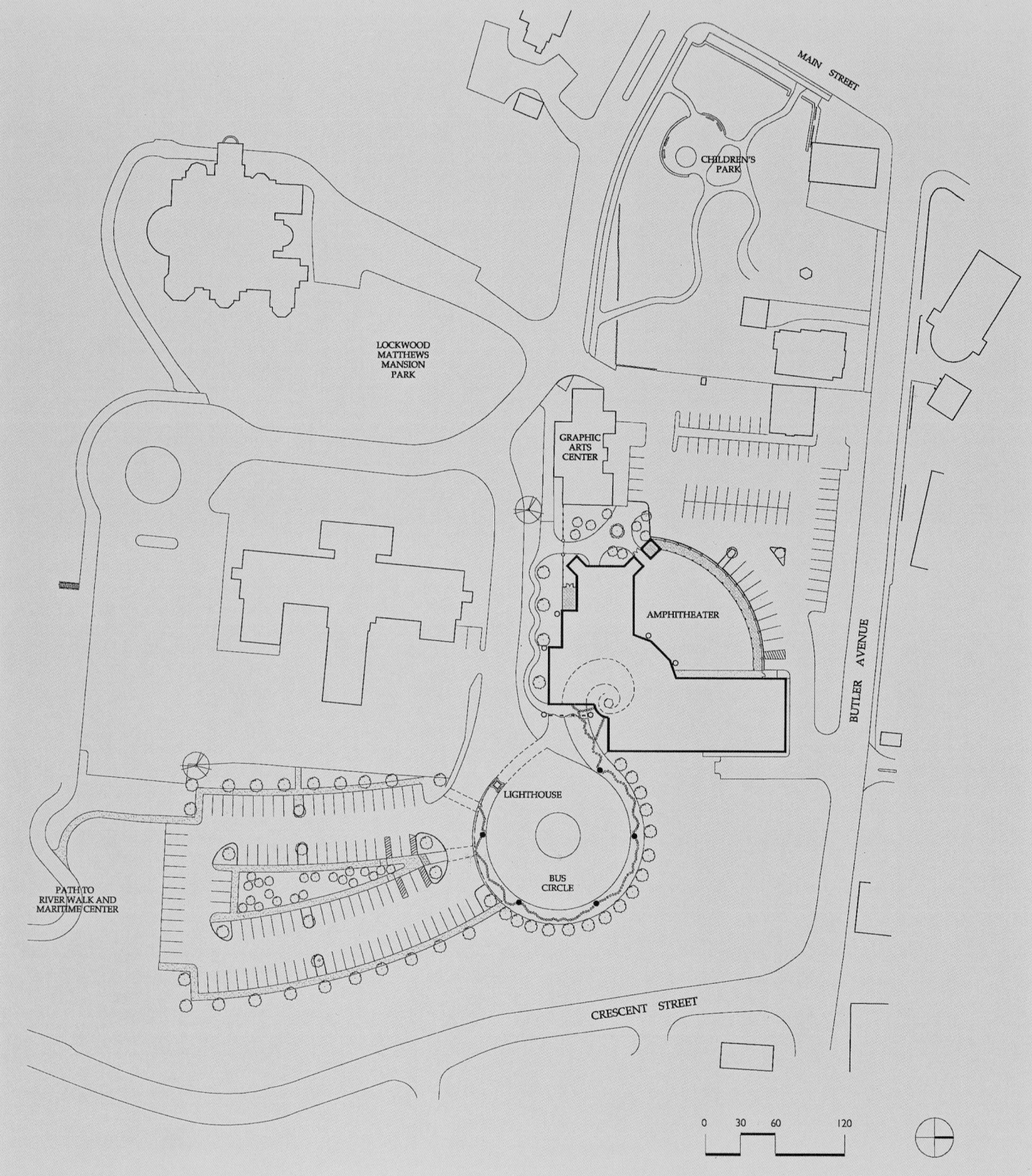

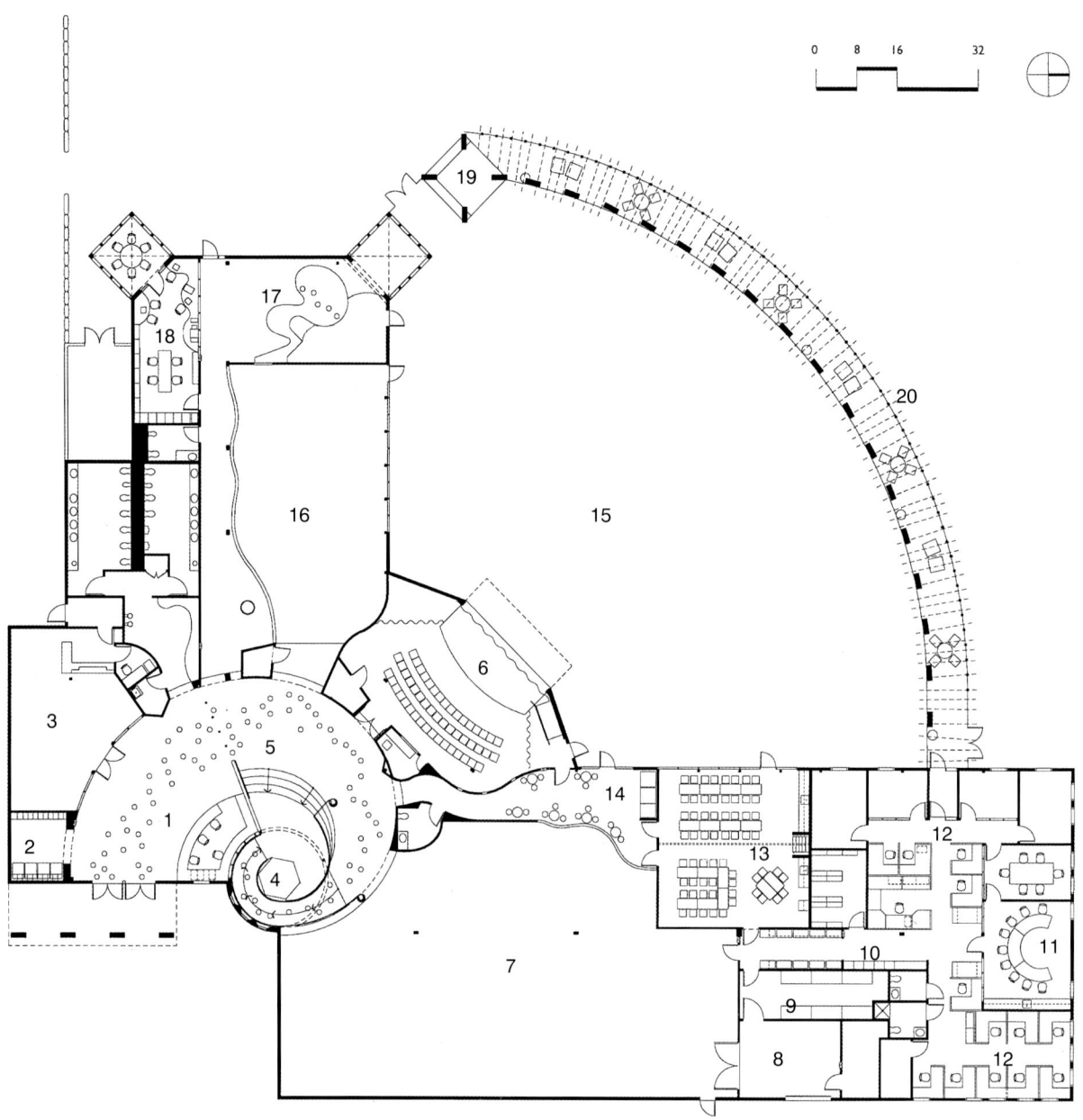

Plan

1. Lobby
2. Coats
3. Gift Shop
4. Tower
5. The Hub
6. Theater
7. Exhibit Gallery
8. Loading
9. Workshop
10. Program Carts
11. Think Tank
12. Offices
13. Multi-purpose room
14. Café
15. Amphitheater and play area
16. Water Gallery
17. Toddler area
18. Resource room
19. Gazebo
20. Pergola

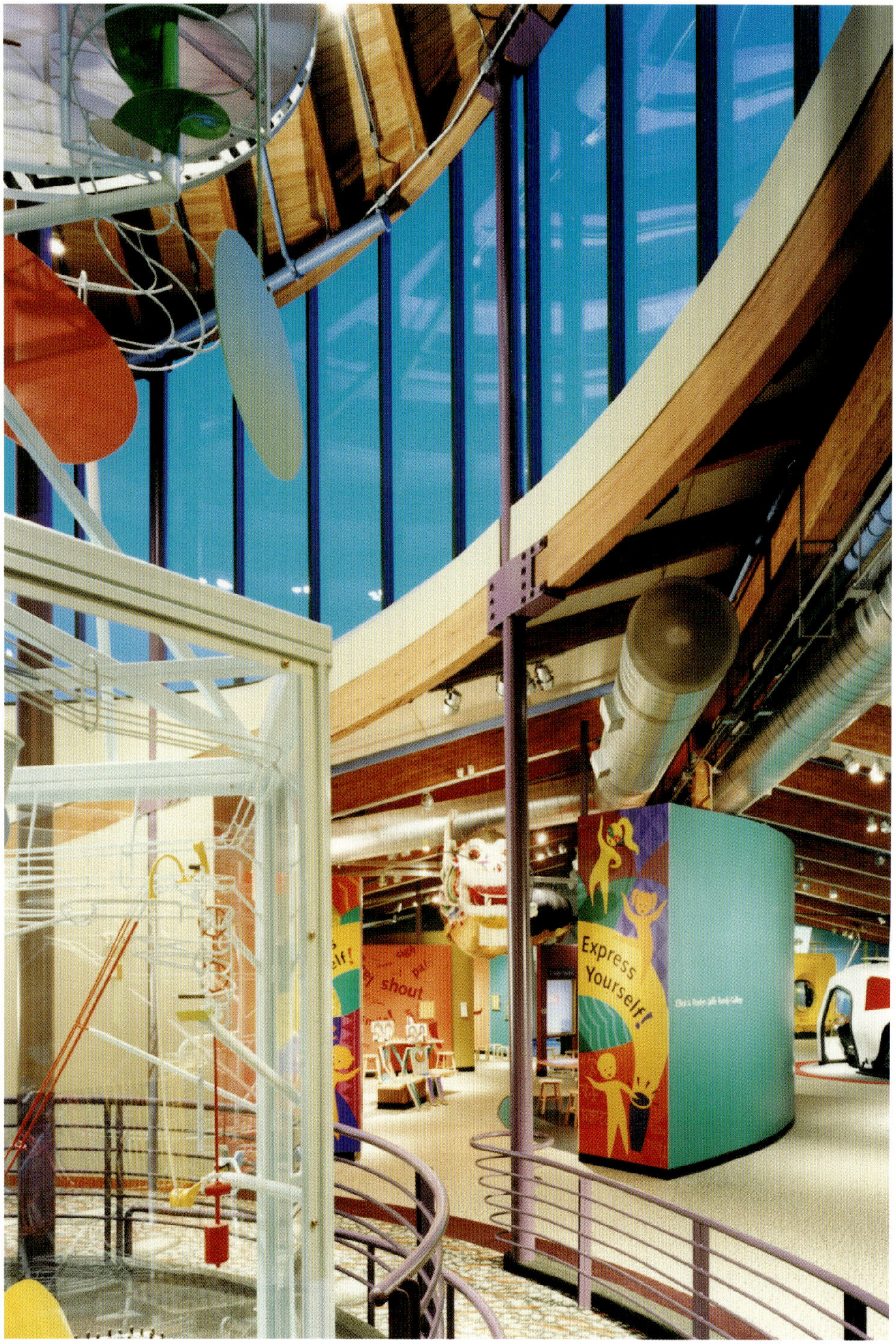
Express Yourself!
shout

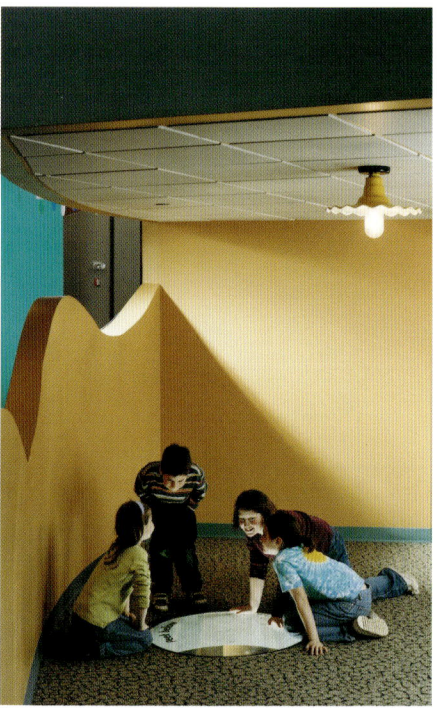

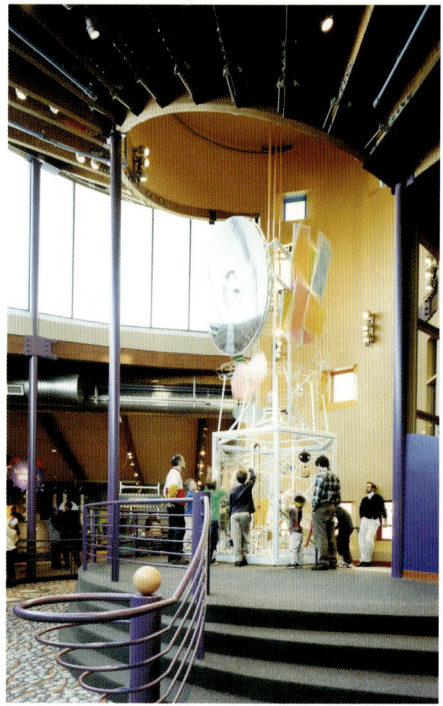

The building is filled with "S" shapes in reference to the museum's name, Stepping Stones. Elements such as the exterior columns, finials, fish in the carpet, paths, roof top birds, table legs, weeping eyes, and hand rails all have the letter "S" in their shapes.

Papalote Childrens Museum
Marinela S. de Lerdo de Tejada - Maribel Ibarra

Mexico, D.F., Mexico

photographs: contributed by Papalote Children's Museum

Eleven years after opening its doors to the public, the Papalote Children's Museum was subjected to an overhaul in order to upgrade its thematic contents as well as its design. The renovation process involved three years of research in conjunction with an English company that contributed valuable tools that enabled the design development and production to be carried out in Mexico by Mexican designers.

Located in the second section of the historical complex of the Chapultepec Forest, the museum is set up as a metaphor of a park – a place where the children own the space, where they instinctively take on activities, play and enjoy themselves in the three main completely renovated sections of the museum: Comunico (I communicate), Soy (I am) and Pertenezco (I belong).

The design of Comunico is a representation of the pond in this imaginary "park", where, like a pebble dropped in water, ripples of "communication" reach even the furthest shore. These circles give rise to basic shapes which house the multi-media computer work stations. Blue, representing water, is the basic color here, accompanied by orange and green accents.

The palette of materials includes frosted plexiglass in orange, green or clear versions, their translucence adding a light touch, combined with stainless steel bases, all coming together to modernize the look of the space.

The exhibits in this zone feature the latest technology, echoing current communications systems that rely on computer programming. Particular emphasis is placed on the importance of having a message, the means of communicating being nothing more than the tool to convey what needs to be said.

The underlying theme of the graphic design is a pixelated representation of the binary system's "0" and "1". It also makes use of lines of "connectivity" and different icons for each activity.

The Soy hall takes its form from the concept of a path running through the park, or the path through this adventure where the children are the heroes of the story, freely choosing the routes they will take through the exhibits. The same materials used in Comunico are present here, but with the color yellow predominating and with the addition of polished vinyl evoking the human figure as the axis of the theme "I am": I am my mind, I am my spirit, I am a part of nature, I am my body and I am a social being.

Pertenezco (I belong) is the "tree" in the park, the house, the refuge: the shapes here are organic figures springing from the leaves and branches of a tree. Green is the color which here complements the basic palette of materials found in the other areas. The design also features elements seen in the other sections, while incorporating colorful details and an abstraction of the "tree of life" in polished vinyl. Tradition and technology are combined in the activities in this section, with children playing timeless childhood games, but using a plasma screen.

The "Biodiversity Hall" combines traditional research methods, but with computer stations and digital microscopes as modern-day tools.

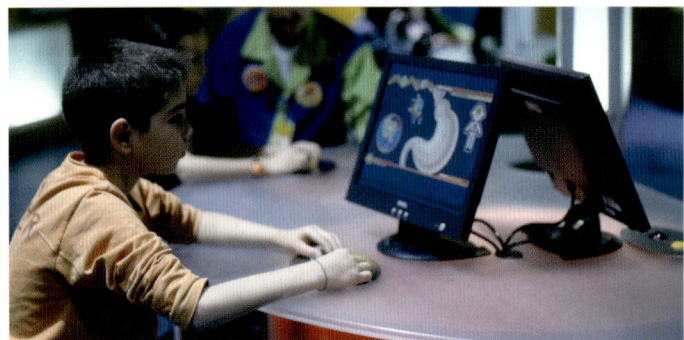

131

Springthorpe Playground
Taylor Cullity Lethlean

Springthorpe Village Green, Melbourne, Australia   photographs: Ben Wrigley

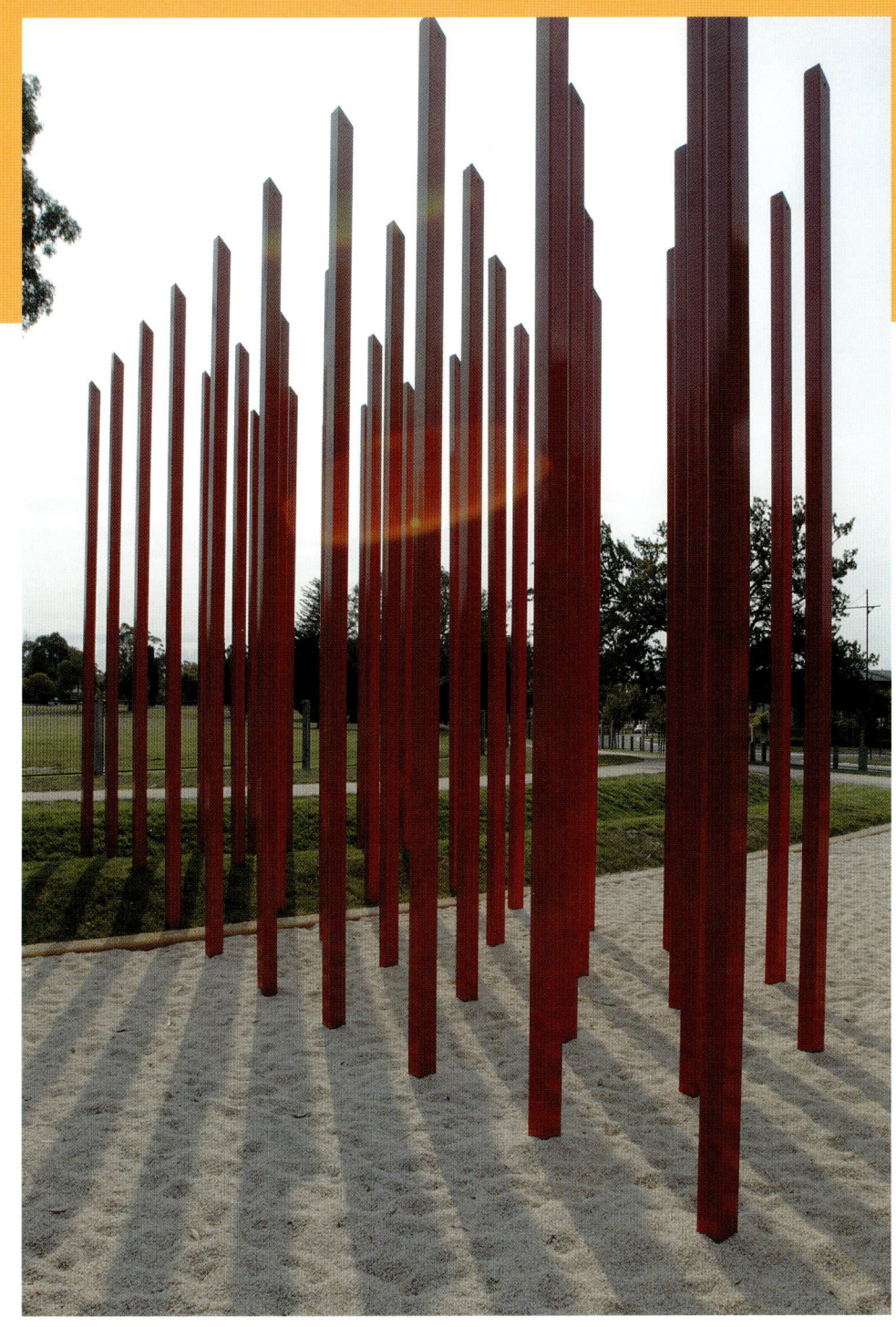

Springthorpe Playground forms one part of an integrated open space network that is part of a large residential development north of Melbourne, Australia.

The playground is located at a principal entry point to the development and connects with other recreational and social community facilities.

The design was conceived as a labyrinth created from the repetition of vertical poles, painted in a vibrant and engaging color. The poles form an oversized forest, partially sunken beneath the adjacent levels, and the armature for containing detailed play elements for senior and junior play.

The formal arrangement creates a sculptural field through which children can chase, hide and explore. Corridors are defined connecting entry points to the play elements. In association with the vibrant red structure, soft surfaces of pea gravel and adjacent rolling lawns create further play opportunities.

Play Structure

Interplay Design & Manufacturing, Inc.

Kannonsaki Park, Kanagawa Prefecture, Japan
Showa Memorial National Park, Tokyo, Japan

photographs: Masaki Koizumi

Originally conceived by the textile artist Toshiko Horiuchi MacAdam, these structures are based on her exploration of the character of fiber and textile structures and on her twenty-five years of experience working with children. The structural analysis and design of the projects has been carried out by Norihide Imagawa of T.I.S. & Partners, Tokyo, Japan.

The modest scale (14m x 10.4m x 3.5m) of the play structure at Kannonsaki park makes it suitable even for very young children, who intuitively understand its potential. The perimeter of the nets varies from only 0.6 to 1.4 meters above ground level, creating a minimal falling hazard. Because its 7 nets are low and interconnected to form a continuous surface, a comparatively light support structure is all that is required.

Using every part of their bodies, children progress from simply trying to gain their balance to jumping, climbing, tumbling, bouncing, swinging and swaying. Even infants and the physically challenged enjoy the rhythmic motion as energy is transmitted through the net.

The scale of the structure at the Showa Memorial is more ambitious. Comprising 63 nets, most of them measuring approximately 5m by 3.5m, this structure can entertain hundreds of children at one time. Measuring 38m x 38m x 5.5m, it incorporates overlapping nets for safety. Each child finds his or her own level of play, although even the adventurous are challenged. Owing to the eccentric loading of the nets and high suspension points, a substantial support structure is required.

The semi-transparent net gives the sensation of floating in space. Its resiliency creates an environment where children of different ages can play together safely.

Stretching and contracting almost like a living organism, the net absorbs energy and releases it, often in unexpected ways that are transmitted throughout the structure.

Kannonsaki Park

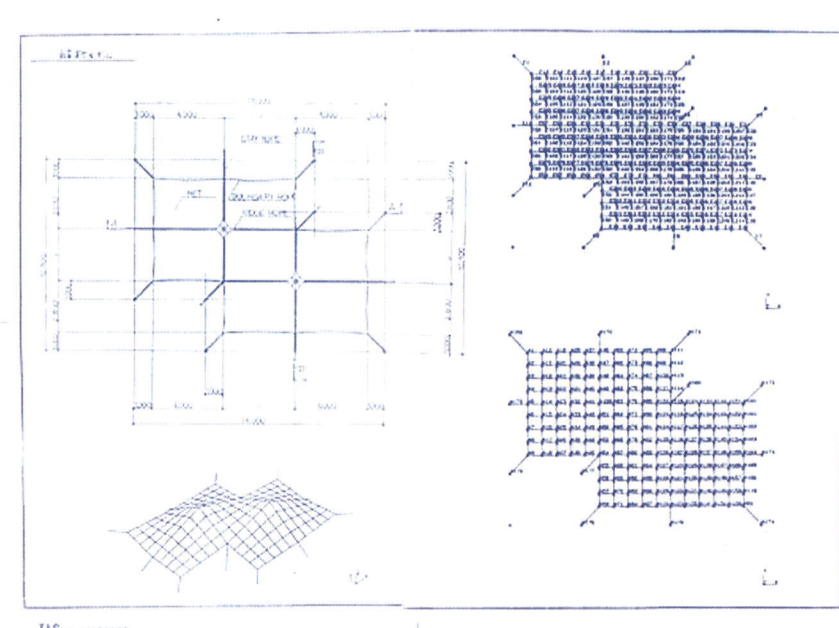

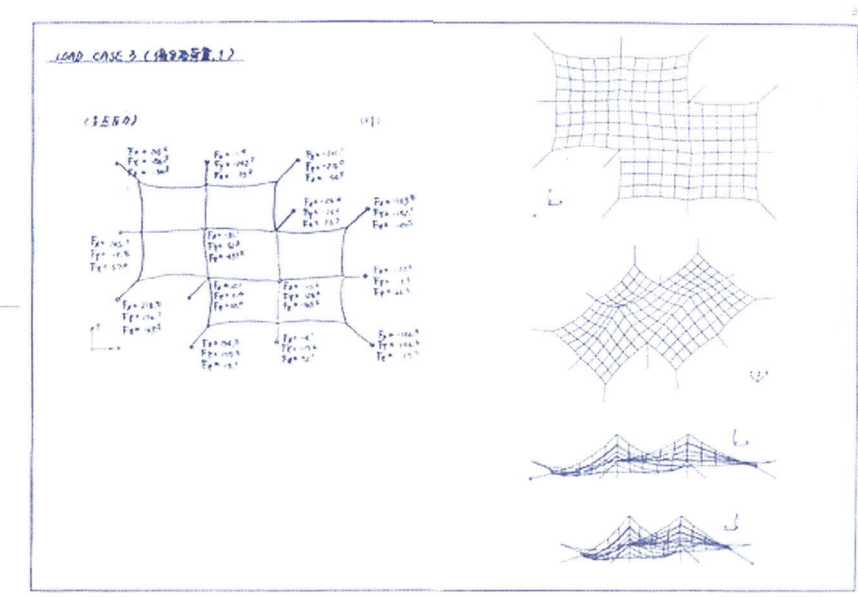

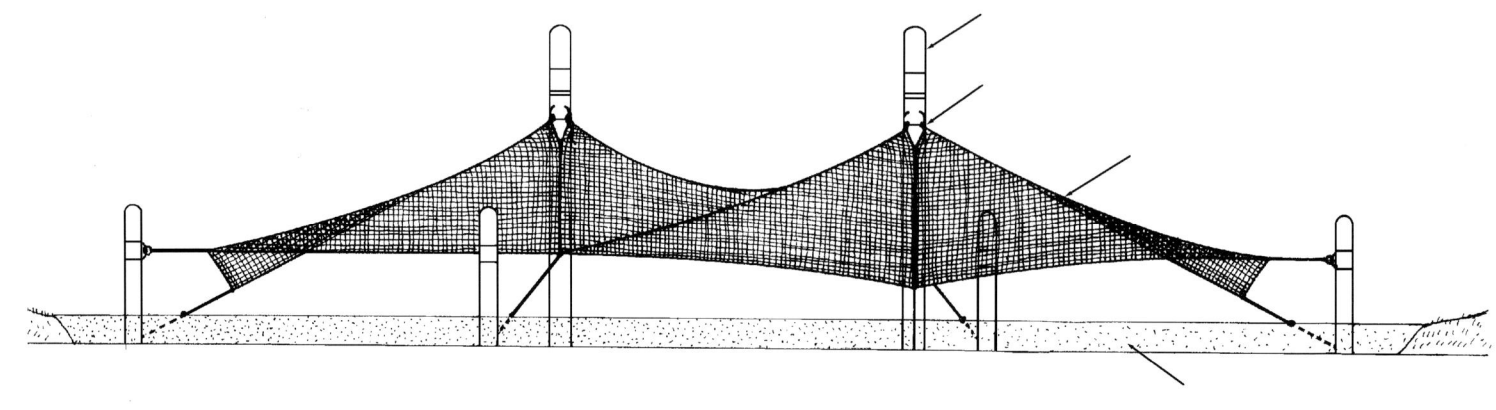
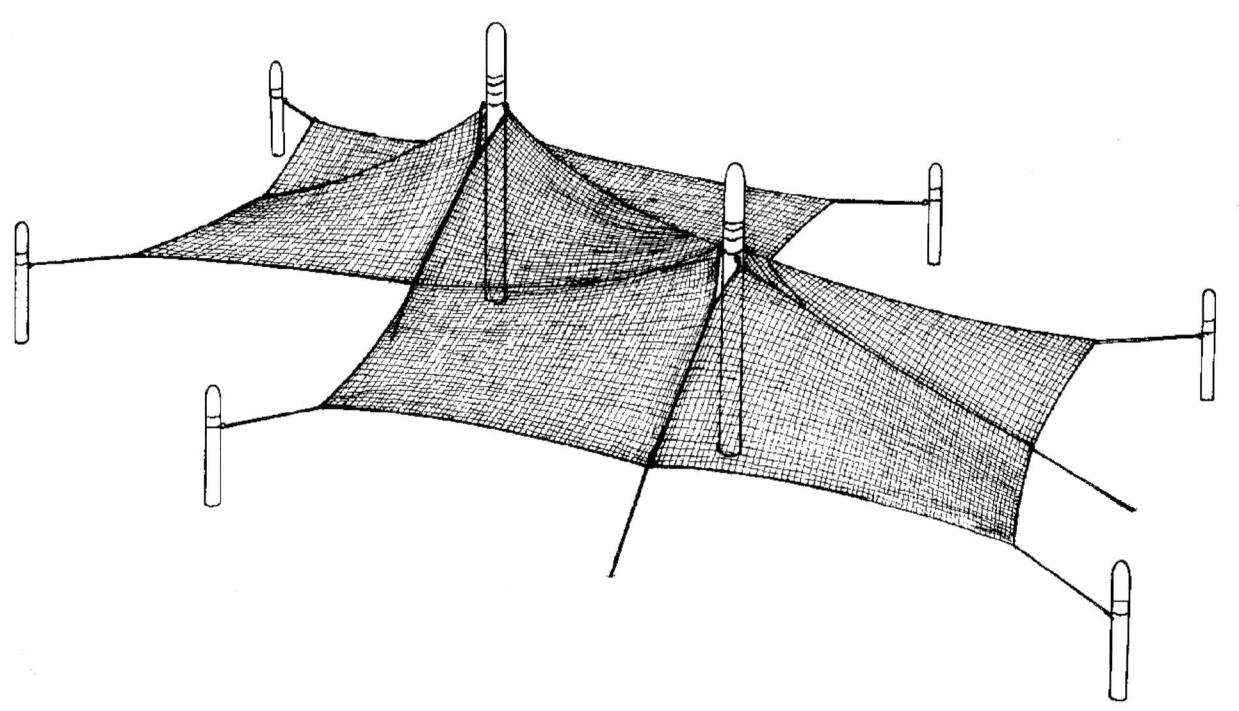

Showa Memorial National Park

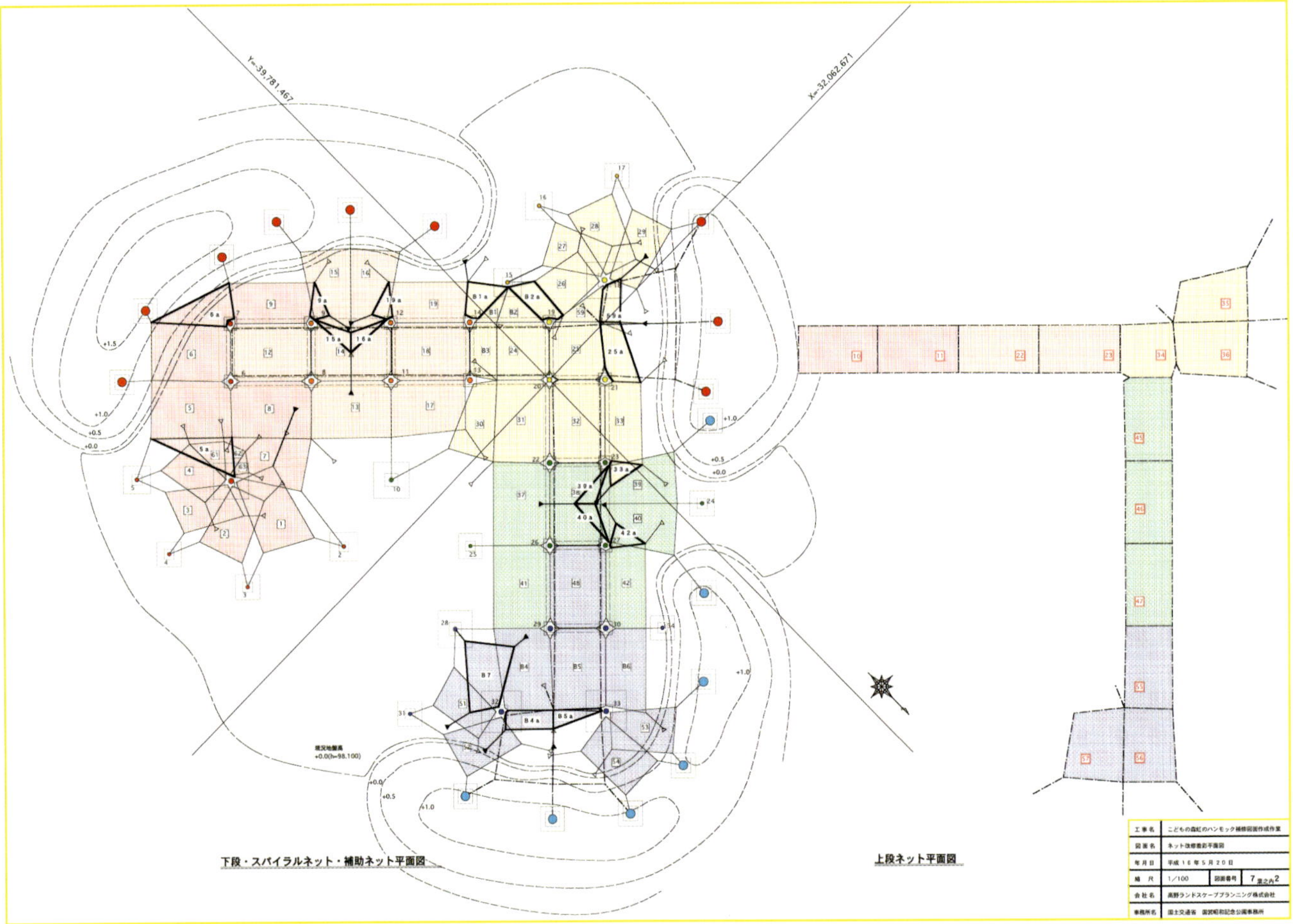

Fair Park Lagoon
Patricia Johanson

Dallas, Texas, USA

photographs: Patricia Johanson

"Fair Park Lagoon", designed in 1981, is the earliest ecological playground in the United States. By providing public access to a functioning swamp in the middle of Dallas' largest public park, Johanson introduces children to living communities and the cycles of nature. The five-block long lagoon is home to native plants and animals in shoreline and aquatic habitats, including snails, clams, freshwater sponges and shrimp, fish, reptiles waterfowl, birds and insects — all of which are both decorative and members of the food chain. Landscaping was conceived of as "food", and sculpture was thought of as not merely "aesthetic", but also as access -- a means of bringing people into contact with the plants, animals, and water.

Paths, bridges, islands, overlooks, and seating were all incorporated into two monumental works of art. At the same time, the "sculpture" was designed as "housing" for animals -- refuges and microhabitats, places to sunbathe and spawn, and protected islands and perches. Planting plans feature plants that grow in shallow water because they provide wildlife food and habitat, help control bank erosion and improve water quality.

"Pteris multifida", a multi-span arch bridge in the form of a fern, creates its own landscape of arches, causeways and islands. Areas of water between the paths form flower basins, fish ponds, and microhabitats. A second sculpture at the opposite end of the lagoon, the Delta Duck Potato "Sagittaria platyphylla", features a mass of twisted "roots" built as five-foot wide paths over the lagoon, with thinner "stems" rising above the water as perches for birds. Floating "leaves" further out in the lagoon become islands for animals, while others along the shore form step seating and overlooks.

The sculptural pathways nestle in two groups at either end of the lagoon and are firmly anchored to the shore. Dividing the pathways into two smaller clusters avoids the formulation of a massive complex, which might be overwhelming, and keeps them instead on a human scale. Though the paths are tangled and some end by sinking into the water, we can see that the extensions are never more than twenty or so paces away from the shore. Psychologically, the feeling of taking a risk while walking out onto water has been kept to a minimum. (Actual risks have been minimized by making the paths comfortably wide with a good grip and putting them in shallow areas of the lagoon.)

The unusual organic forms and vibrant terra cotta color of Johansons's paths can be seen from a great distance, especially as they are surrounded by bright green plants. Once out over the water, the sculpture disappears underfoot and the focus shifts to a dragonfly, a fairy shrimp, a spawning fish, or a water lily. The sculptural, curvilinear forms at varying gradients and heights, like a highway ramp, forces people to slow down and watch their step, making them more attentive to their surroundings.

Because the structures are based on actual plants, people who walk the paths can follow the same curves and rhythms as the biological forms, repeating the pattern of the plant. The rich variety of details at the lagoon is only revealed through time and movement-- incorporating the fluctuating water levels and the life and death cycles that constantly alter the appearance of the lagoon.

155

Aichi Children's Center

Mitsuru Senda + Environment Design Institute

Nagakute Town, Aichi, Japan

photographs: Mitsumasa Fujitsuka

Constructed inside Aichi Prefecture's Nagakute Youth Park, this is Japan's largest children's facility. The "play atrium" is encircled at its top part by a corridor for play equipment, in addition to an architectural corridor. At the center part, a tower-like construction of play equipment called the "Challenge Tower" sustains the large Teflon roof with a double helical flow line.

Overall, it comprises a wide assortment of different play equipments assembled under the shelter of the giantumbrella, a contained circle for play, games and experience. Its use value has been further enhanced by a large adjucent space containing training, development, trial and experiment facilities related to the monitoring, design and care of play zones.

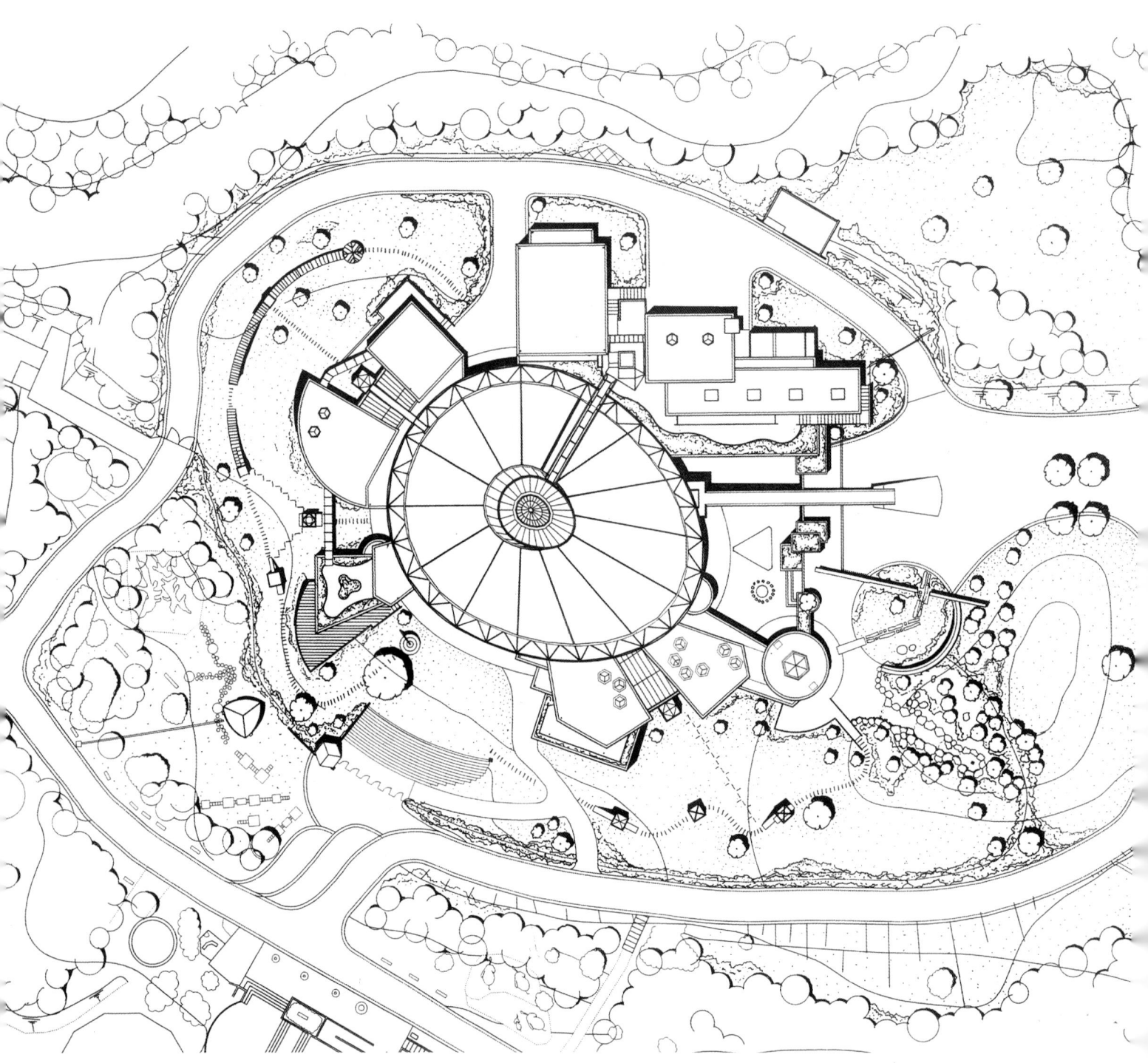

163

164

Parque de la Ribera

Kompan

Bilbao, Spain

photographs: contributed by Kompan

This spectacular play space is covered in 1800 square meters of continuous impact-absorbent safety flooring. The architectonic layout was conceived from the outside in – that is, from the surrounding context inward, respecting the general alignment of the park's spatial scheme while analyzing how each sector is accessed, where it could be opened up or enclosed, where sitting areas should be set up and which views should be enhanced.

Abandoibarra was a defunct industrial port zone in the city's center. The renovation of this area and subsequent recuperation of the urban waterfront was considered a symbol of the regeneration of the city of Bilbao. The area is bounded by the Guggenheim museum, set in the former naval shipyards and the Euskalduna Palace.

From the outset, the city council aimed to recover the watercourse for public use via an organized transformation of the new space that would thereby be gained.

In order to enhance the process of recuperating the waterfront zone, the underlying principle of the design process was that it should be particularly alluring to people passing by on foot. This idea naturally led to the understanding that the area should necessarily include a playground.

Bearing the long-term goals in mind, conventional solutions were immediately ruled out, with the designers aiming instead for a modernized solution, both in the play options that children would be offered as in the applied construction technology.

The play spaces have been designed as a unified architectonic piece within the complex of the Parque de Abandoibarra, creating a highly expressive foot path between two of the city's most emblematic landmarks: the Guggenheim and the Palacio de Congresos y de la Música, while at the same time resolving the link between the waterway and the urban fabric.

The act of regeneration was, and continues to be, carried out in the entire Abandoibarra zone. The fact that the play area sits closer to the Guggenheim was determined by the greater availability of space in that area.

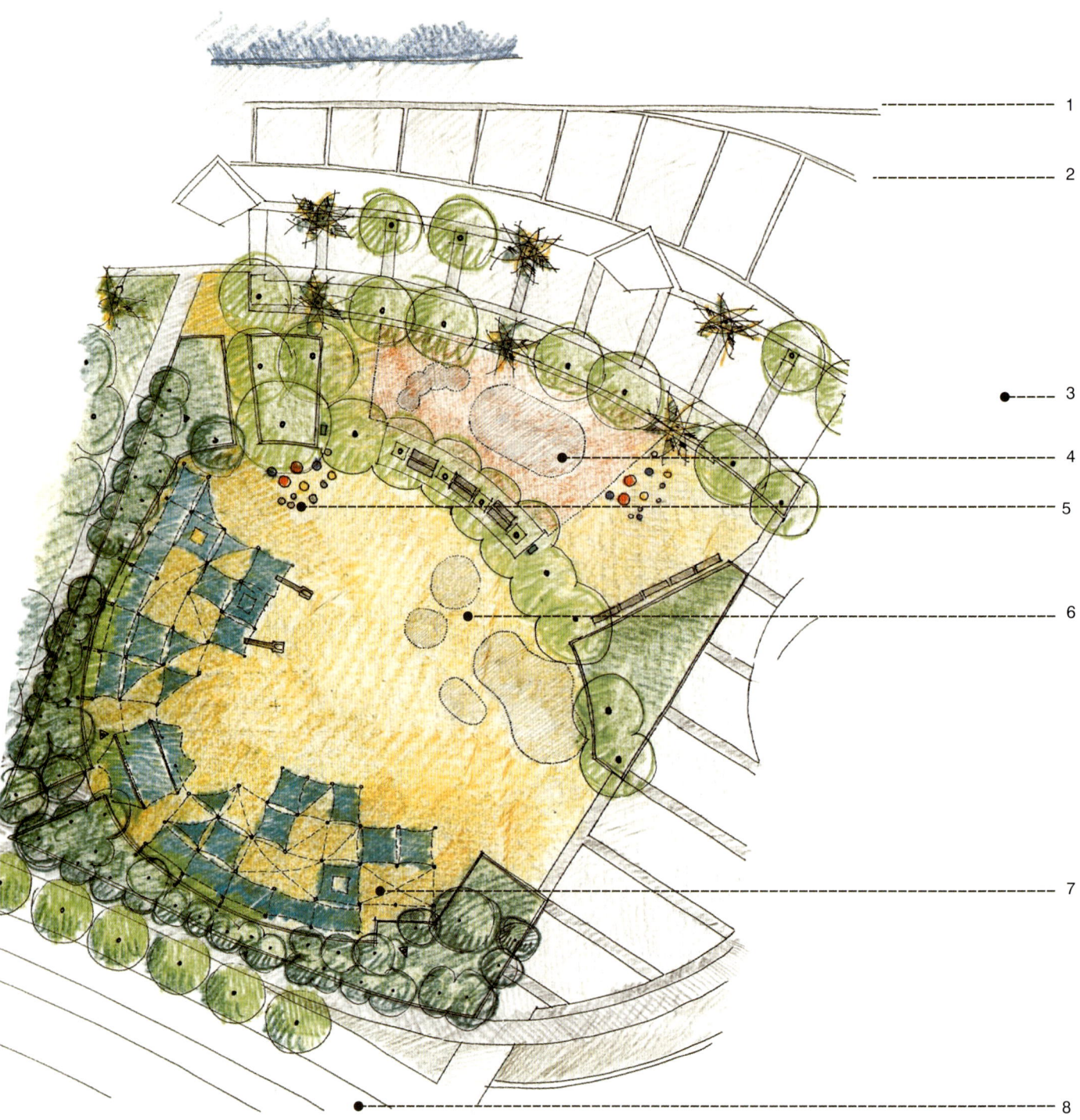

Ground plan

1. Nervión estuary
2. Paseo (Avenue) del Bajo
3. Esplanade of the Guggenheim Museum
4. Moments / Elements play area
5. Field of spheres
6. Galaxy play area
7. Corocord play area, Pilonas Forest
8. Paseo (Avenue) del Alto

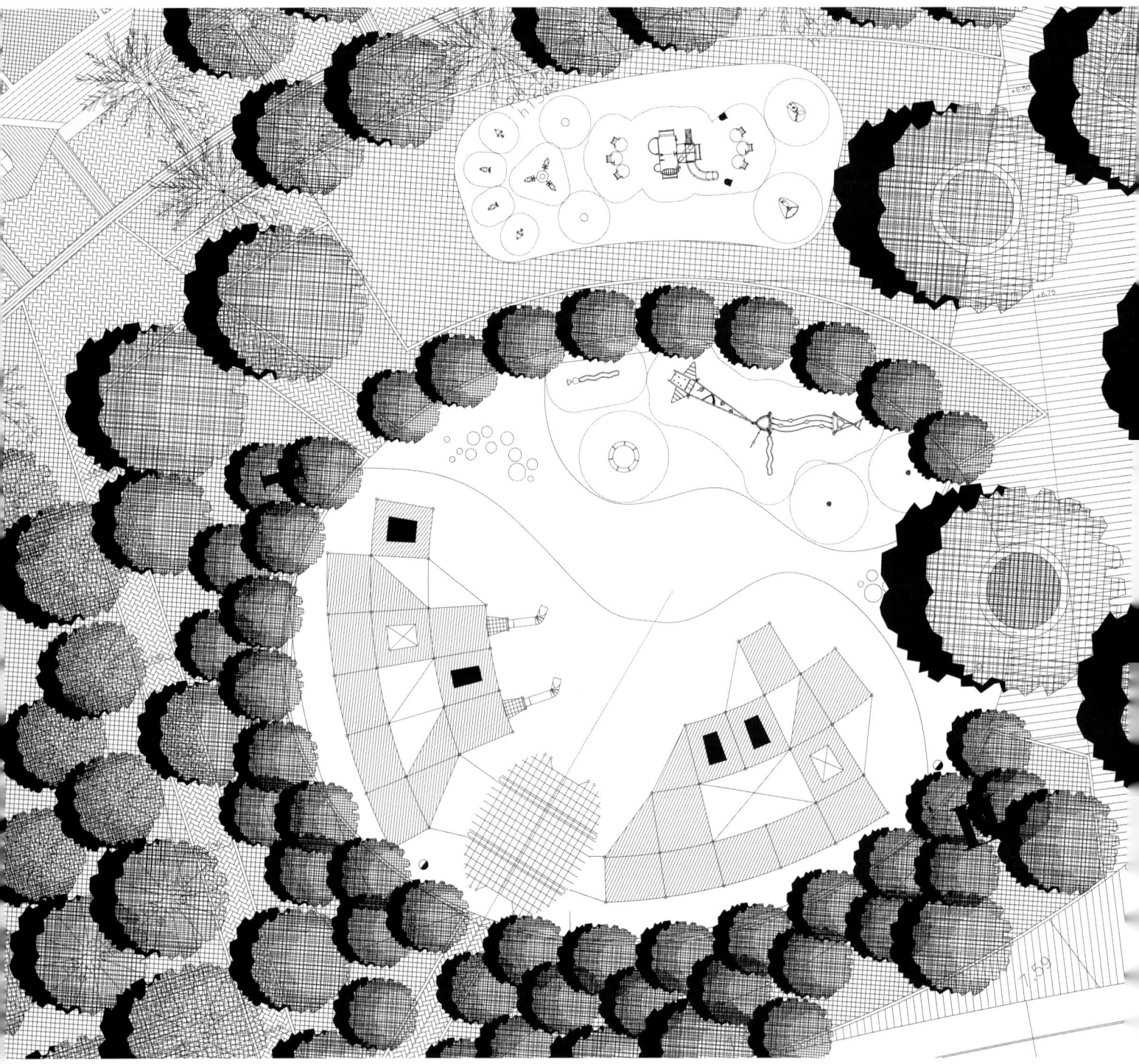

Eureka! The Museum for Children SoundSpace
Northern Light CoDesign

Halifax, UK

photographs: contributed by Erueka!

Eureka!, the UK's first and foremost museum for children, recently launched this new interactive music gallery utilizing state-of-the-art interactive technology, designed especially for children aged 3-12. SoundSpace provides children with a truly unique experience by enabling them to explore the science behind sound, music and performance.

SoundSpace is an innovative collaboration between the acclaimed sound artist Thor McIntyre-Burnie and Dutch exhibition designers Northern Light CoDesign. The groundbreaking new gallery covers approximately 500 square meters to replace the existing Invent, Create, Communicate gallery on the ground floor, with a series of 21st century hands-on exhibits representing the cutting edge of children's exhibition design.

Thor McIntyre Burnie comments: "This collaboration is an unprecedented step for all involved - no other children's museum has invited an artist to have creative input into an interpretation strategy on this scale."

Groups of children can embark upon an amazing journey of discovery to help a young visiting alien from a faraway planet explore music and learn about the key elements of which it is composed.

Throughout the experience, SoundSpace aims to enhance the understanding of Science, Technology, Engineering and Math (STEM) by exploring the unique relationships that exist between music and creativity, science, technology and the arts in a fun and accessible way.

Orby the Alien introduces and guides the children throughout each of the 8 gallery zones, beginning with: Trans-Portal, where children learn about the Golden Record released into space by NASA in 1977 on the Voyager spacecraft and how Orby the Alien finds the record and wants to discover more about the intriguing music and voices from planet earth, setting out to find the answers at Eureka!.

The next gallery, Sound Sampler, is a spiral of sound-interactive activities that explore the science of sound enabling children to see and feel vibrations, experiment with sources of sound, volume, pitch and giant instruments. A music matrix with flashing patterns will revolutionize the way music is created, by allowing children to generate their own unique musical compositions and select how they wish their music to look and sound.

In the Orby Theatre children can join in an interactive stage show complete with dramatic sound and lighting to help introduce Orby to the theater and the art of performance.

Continuing the tour is the Control Deck, where users can experiment with sound and lighting effects backstage to interact with live performances on the stage by altering the mood and atmosphere on a mini stage set. In another gallery, Morph Machine, visitors to the museum can experiment with costume and make-up design to create different characters.

The Sound Lounge is a space for investigating the reception of sound and how we react to different types of music, including how different creatures sense vibration and have different hearing ranges. After this, children can take part in a musical journey around the world and find out how music is used in global celebrations at the gallery entitled Orby Mobile.

Finally, in Mix It!, children can become DJ's by mixing and sampling a collection of sounds inspired by nature, to make their own personal hit track.

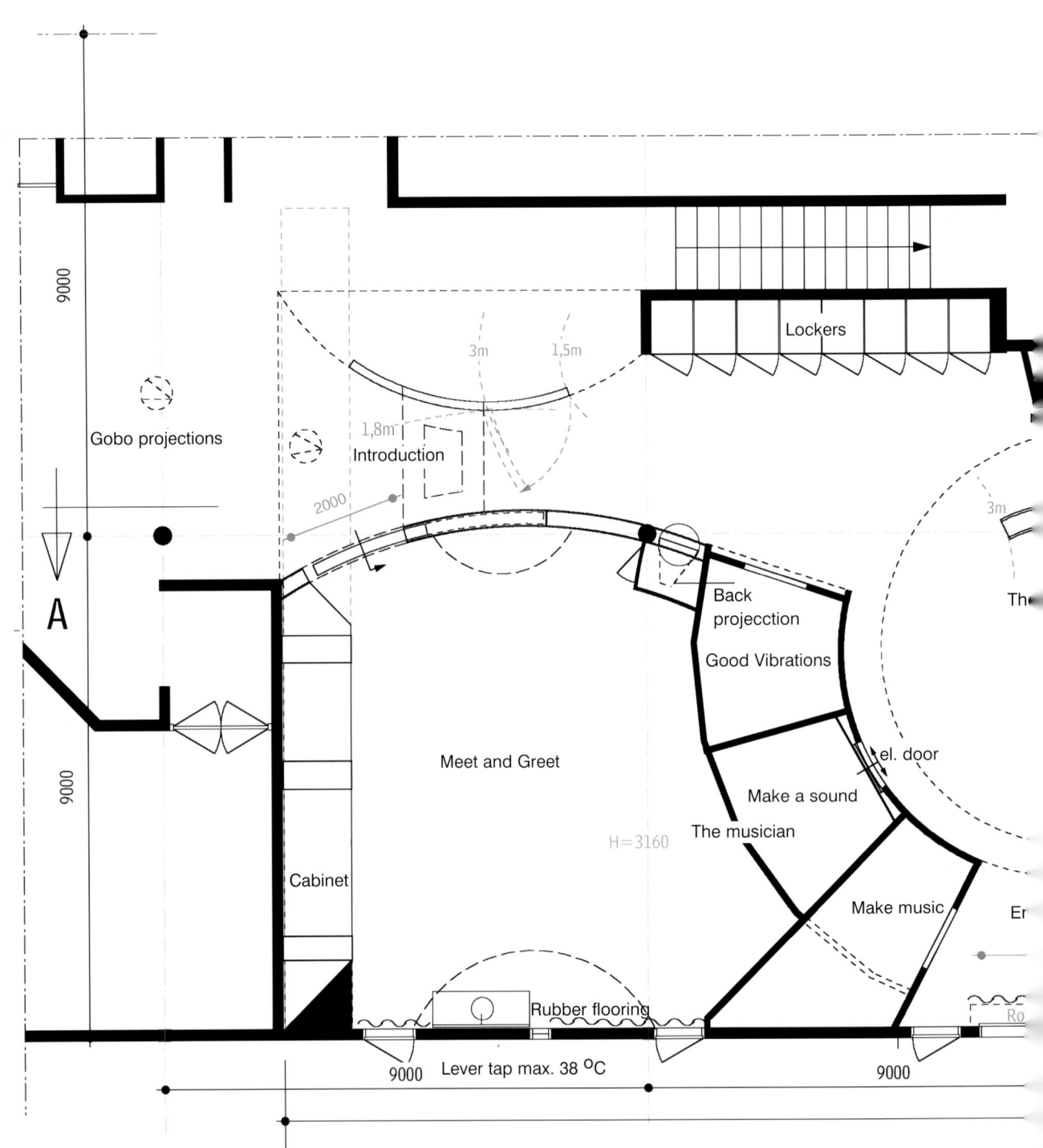

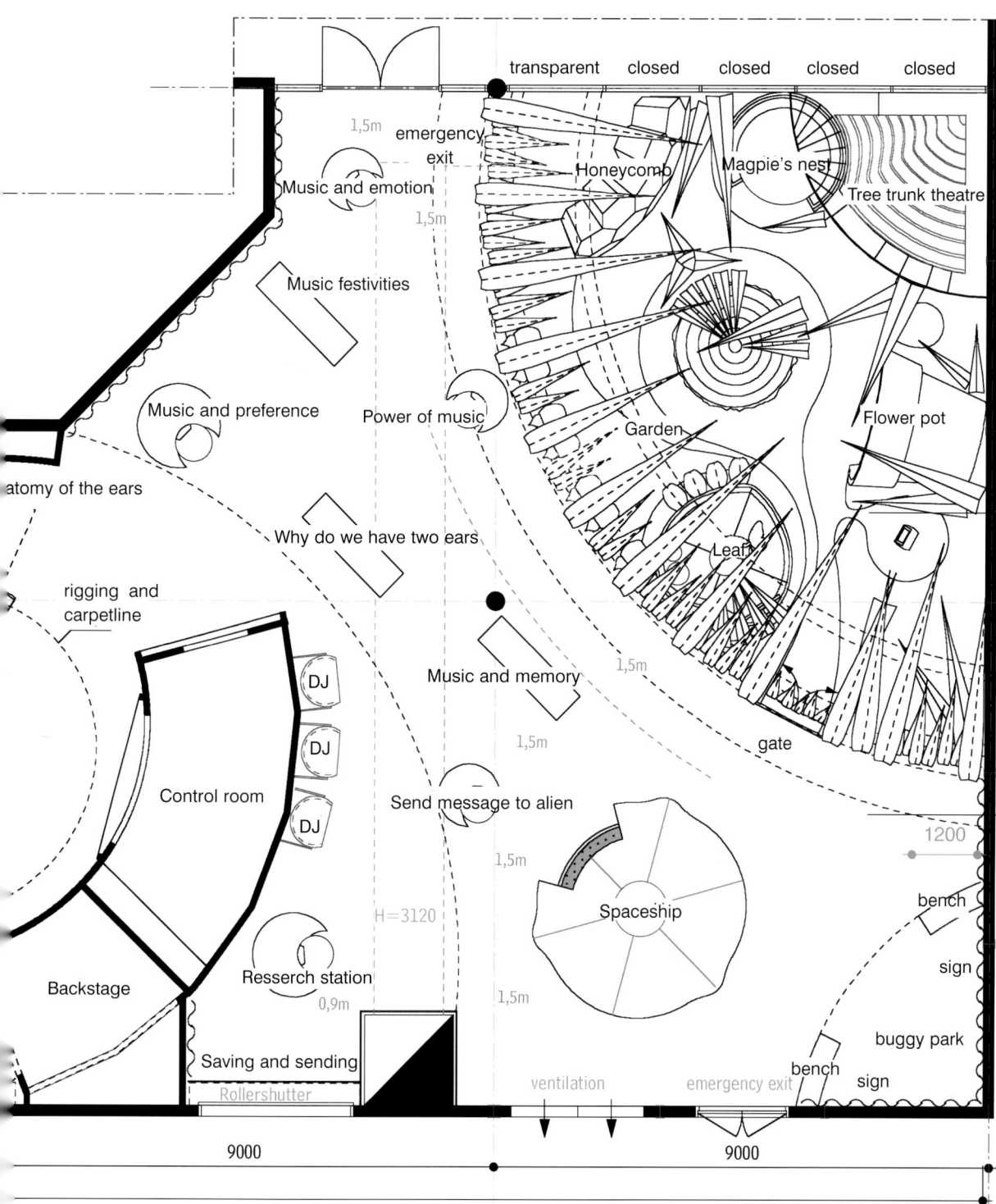

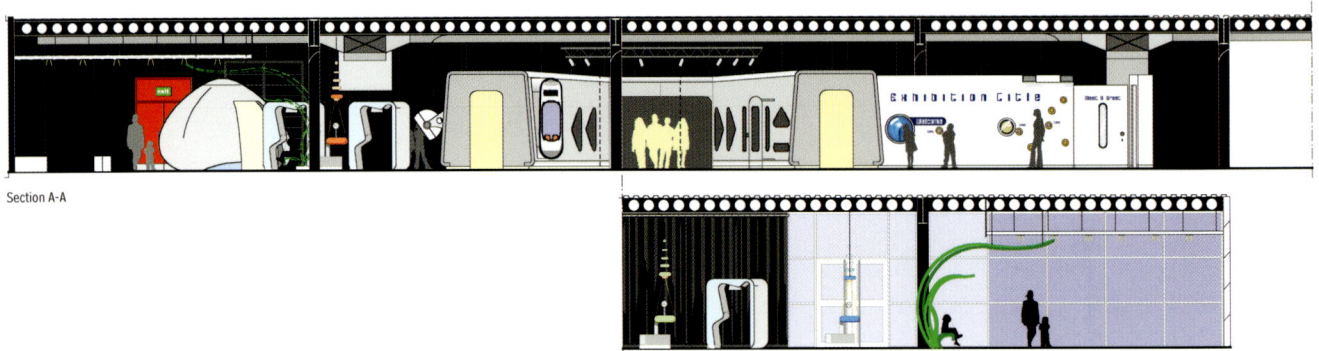

Section A-A

Section B-B

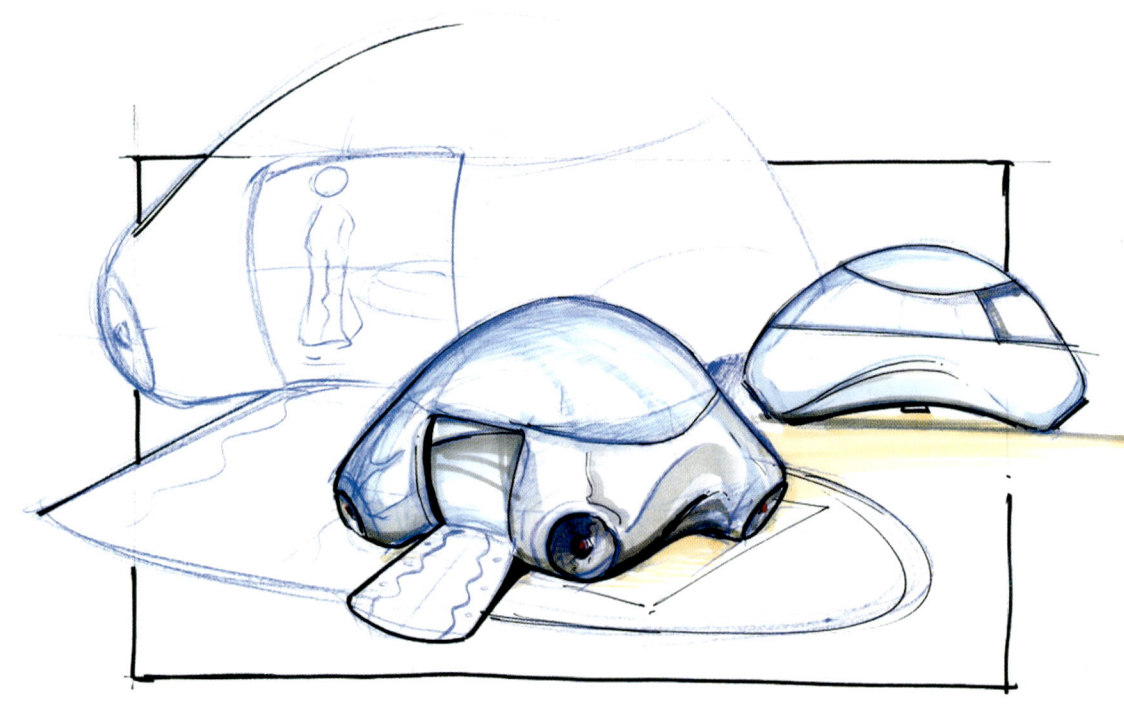
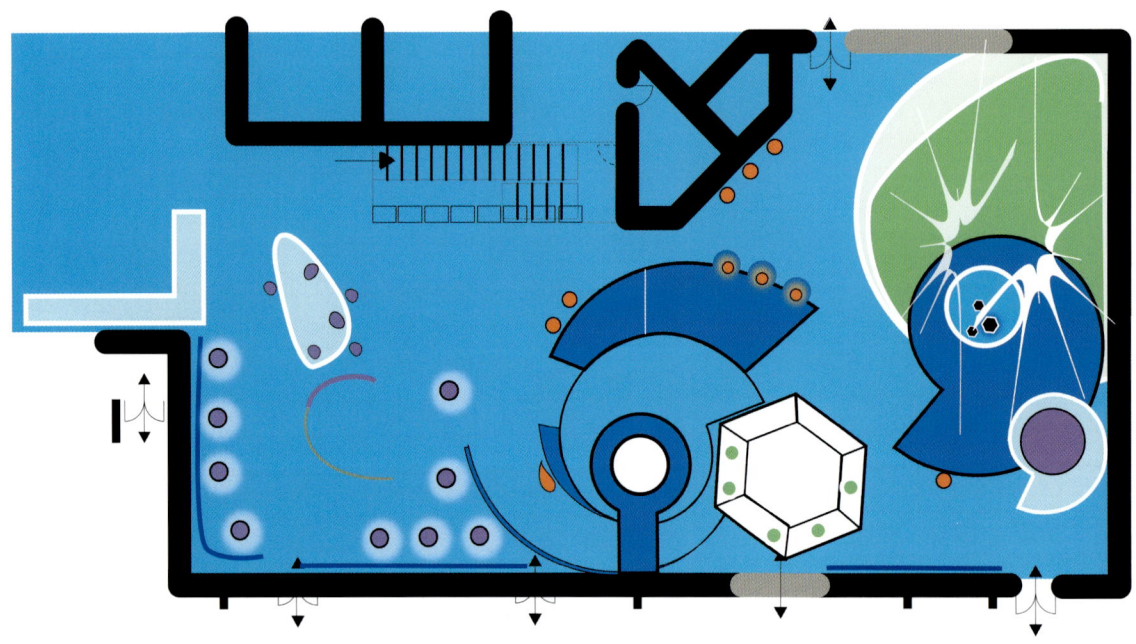

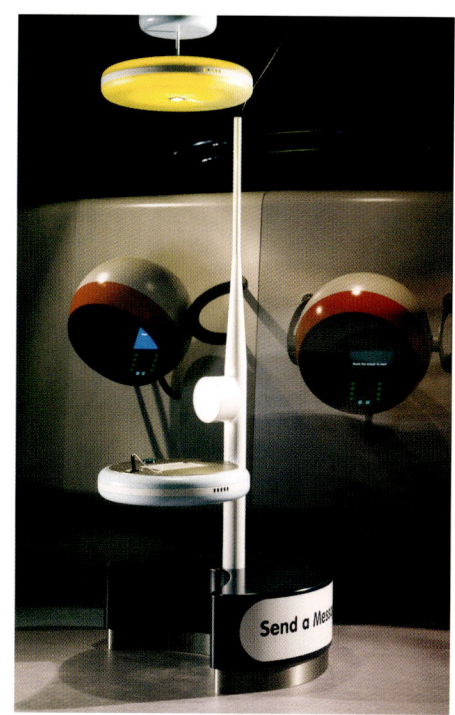
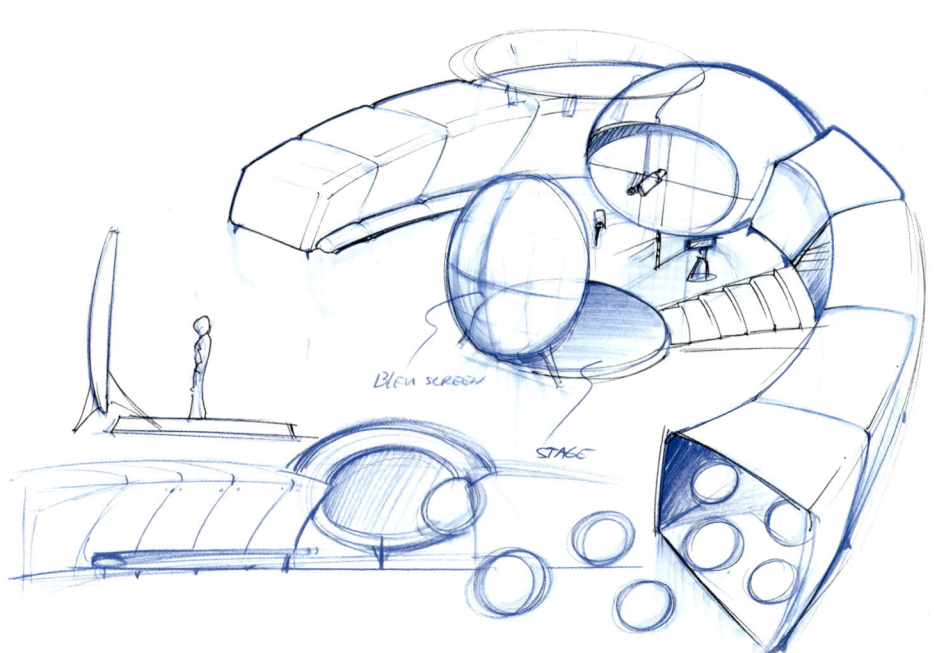

183

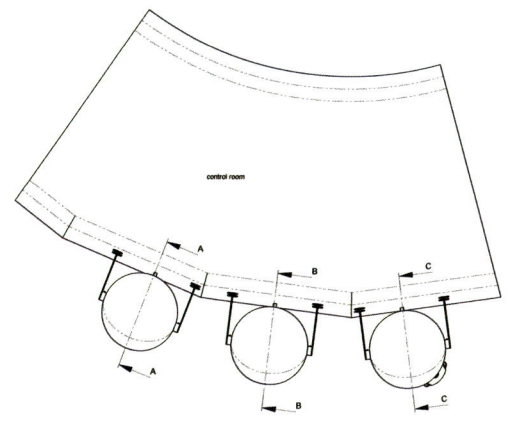
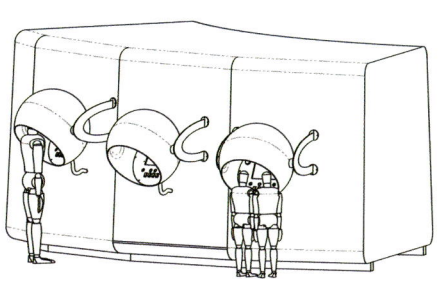
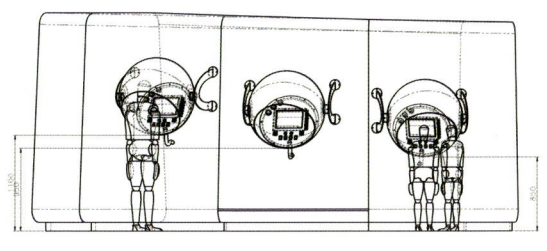
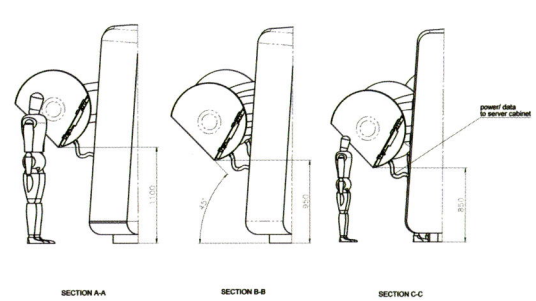

SECTION A-A   SECTION B-B   SECTION C-C

Wooden Playthings

Atsugi Civil Engineering Division & Tokio LAndsc. Architects Inc.

Noyama-kita City Park, Tokyo, Japan   photographs: Kazuyuki Inoue. Sakae. Co. Ltd.

This "playground in the forest" is located to the east of Tokyo's Noyamakita Rokudoyama park. The playground itself occupies an area of 4 hectares within the 256 hectares of the forested park and features a wide range of play equipment scattered here and there among the trees. In clear consonance with the surroundings, the play equipment has been built from wood and natural materials and has also been designed to emulate images and shapes found in nature. Children can hide inside wooden "shells" patterned after the kind of nuts commonly found in the forest or they can slide down a particularly long slide that winds sinuously down between the trees. The tiniest tots can swing in baskets hanging from the trees and the most daring kids can put their physical skills (especially balance and strength) to the test by climbing to considerable heights on "spider webs" and wooden structures with ropes.

This project won the 2001 design award from the Japanese Institute of Landscape Design.

DuPage Children's Museum
architectureisfun, Inc.

Naperville, Illinois, USA

photographs: Doug Snower Photography

Transforming a commercial lumber company into a thoughtful and efficient children's museum was not an easy task, but the collaboration between Peter J. Exley Architect/architectureisfun and Nagle Hartray Danker Kagan McKay Architects Planners Ltd. combined the necessary talent and expertise.

Working closely with both the museum staff and the City of Naperville, the design team developed a comprehensive master plan, which includes future growth, connections to mass transit, and complete accessibility for the disabled.

Face-to-face interviews with children and the important adults in their lives provided the impetus for the initial design. Children drew the new museum as they envisioned it. Their drawings helped in a remarkable way to clarify the master-planning framework as well as to identify some design details that appeared often in the drawings, highlighting just how important they were to the children. The design team also met with staff and outside arts, education, and science advisors.

From kids' drawings to delightful design, Phase One of the planning process takes advantage of existing features such as high ceilings and concrete framing. New interior columns even reach like children's outstretched arms propping up the building – the whimsical result of added bracing to the structural system.

For an institution that kindles curiosity and creativity, it is critical that the architecture also provide stimulation and excitement. The design is child-like, yet sophisticated, and includes 20 different colors of paint, colored lights suspended in playful patterns, and a tactile wall that engages even the youngest children as they walk through the corridor. Because children are tough end-users, materials were chosen as much for their durability as for their color range.

The museum is very interested in self-directed play. Children are provided the space to build their own experiences – with safety in mind. Exley feels that the Construction House, for example, not only gives children the freedom to use real equipment (like nails, saws, hammers, and safety goggles), but also provides a safe environment and encourages important skills.

Bubbles is a perennial favorite and typically a maintenance worry. Huge car wash brushes, like enormous totems, delineate the zone – and keep the bubbles where they belong. Children also love to wipe their hands on them and squeeze their bodies in-between two brushes, some of which were planned deliberately too close to each other. The concrete flooring and rubber mats are durable and easy to maintain.

Children are blown away by AirWorks. The 6-foot-diameter transparent wind tunnel allows air to become a force in a child's life. Outside the tunnel, everyone can watch the child experiment by throwing a Frisbee or by flying streamers and kites. In Make It Move, there's a lot of pushing, dropping, rolling, and pulling going on. Children use energy and coordination to focus on the laws of motion. The Exley team designed inclined walls, climb-throughs, planes, and ramps to move bodies and balls through and around.

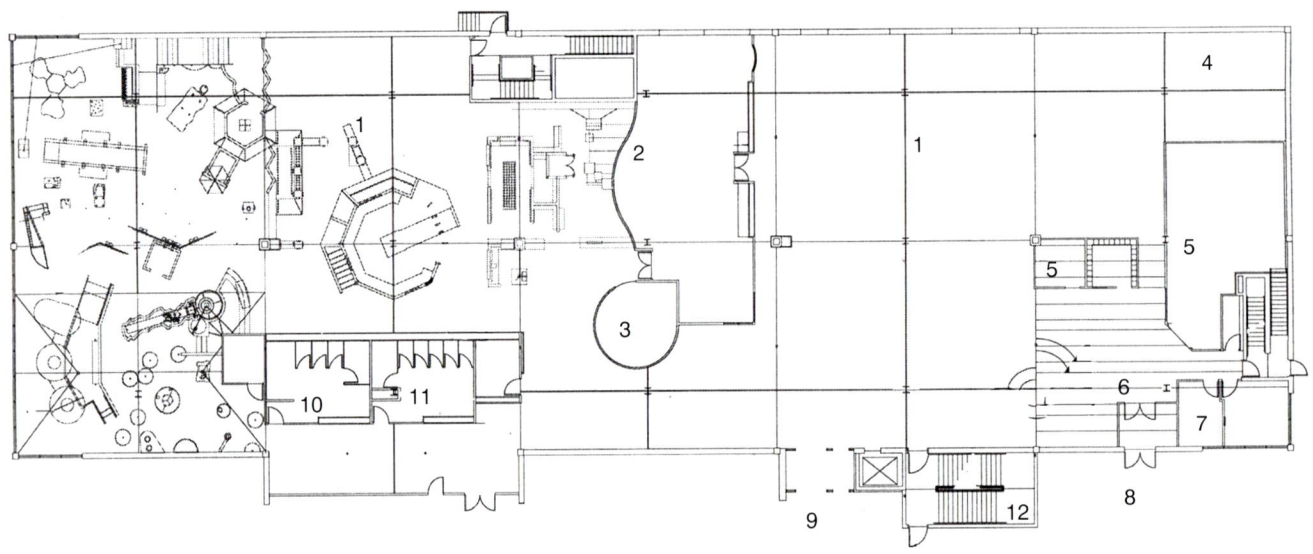

Ground floor plan

1. Exhibit Zone
2. Multi-purpose room/ Art Studio
3. Quiet Room
4. Storage
5. Retail
6. Reception
7. Floor staff
8. Main Entry
9. Group Entry
10. WC Boys
11. WC Girls
12. Stair:
to lower level Exhibit Zone, fabrication shop, storage, school labs.
to second level Exhibit Zone, multi-purpose/event rooms, administrative offices, roof garden.

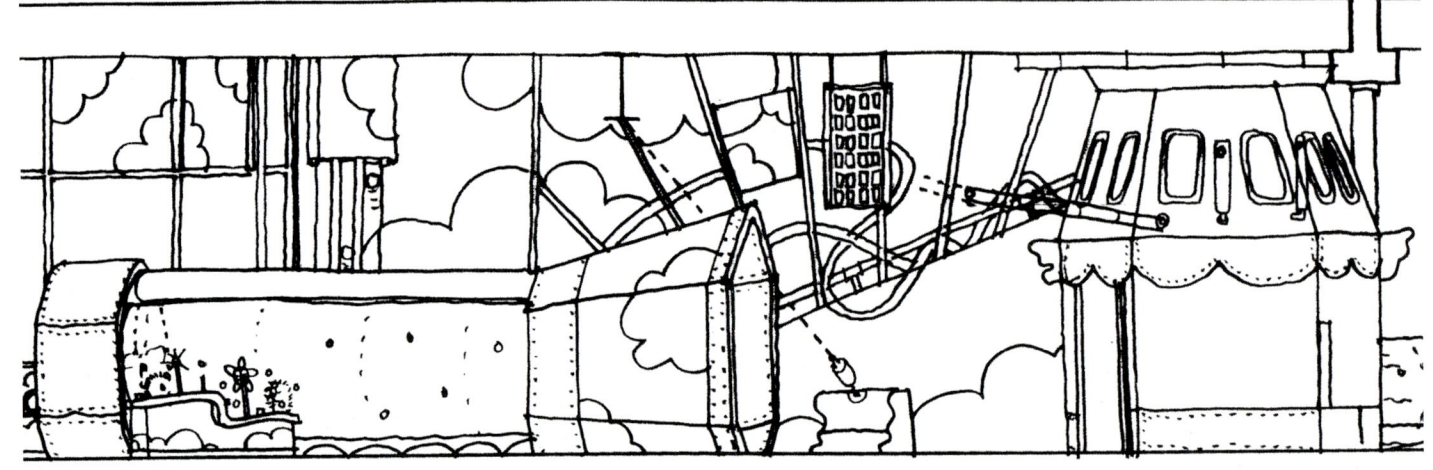

H2O

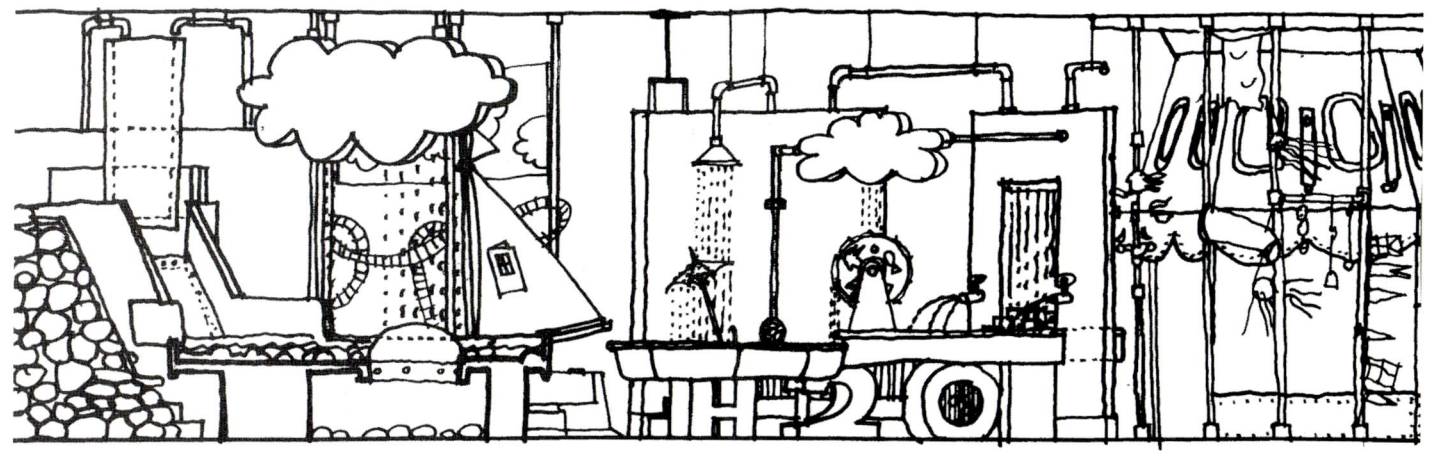

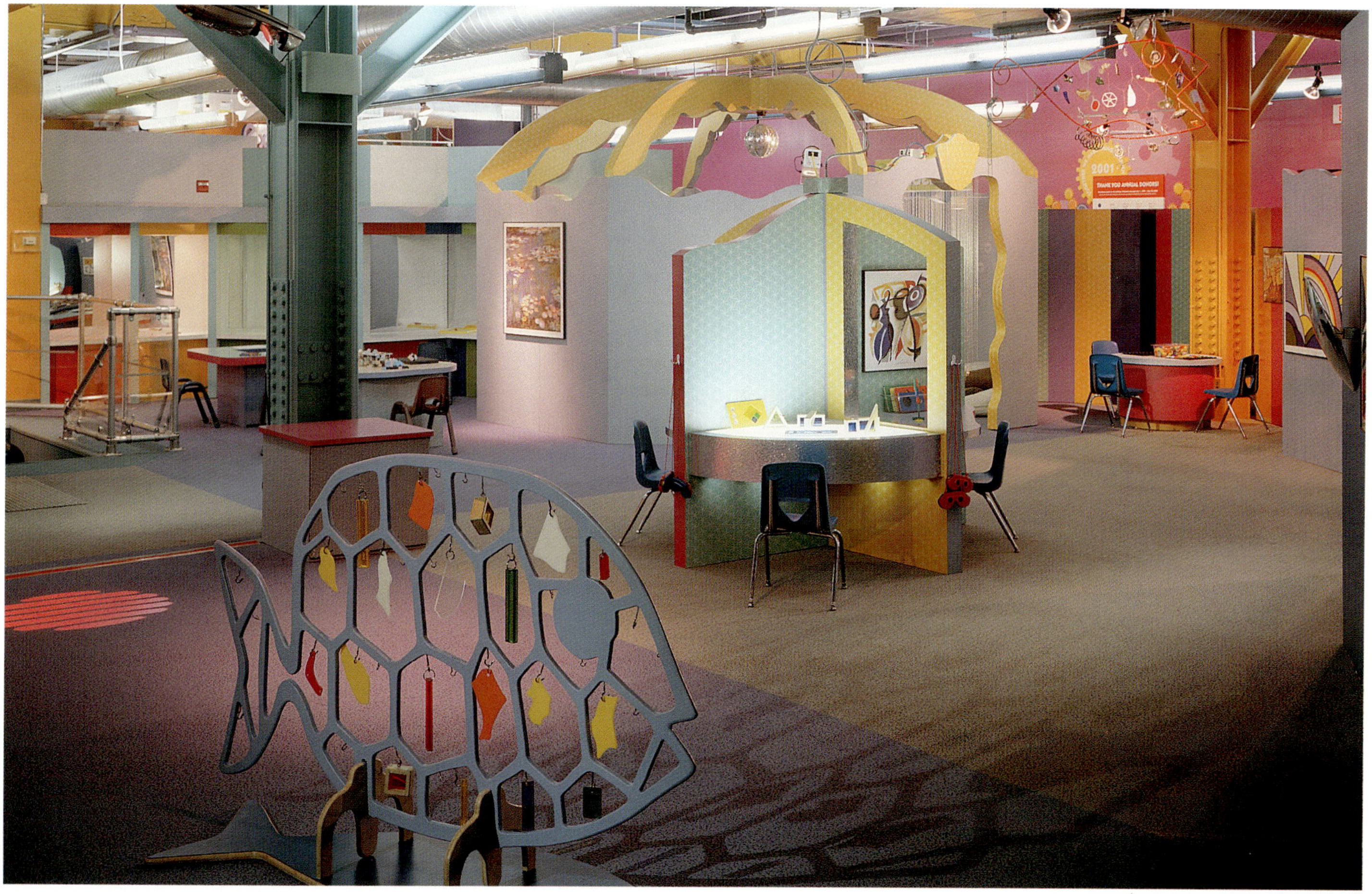
2001
THANK YOU ANNUAL DONORS!

Tea Tree Gully
Taylor Cullity Lethlean & Mary Jeavons

Tea Tree Gully, South Australia, Australia **photographs: Taylor Cullity Lethlean**

The character of this playground is in keeping with the natural setting of its well-treed site. For instance, a whimsical maze of poles topped by decorative metal birds' heads mimics the form of the surrounding forest so perfectly that it almost seems part of the forest itself. Furthermore, the color scheme displays a sense of restraint, providing just enough color to add a touch of playfulness but not so much as to clash with the natural tones of the surroundings.

The palette of materials and equipment is deliberately simple, trusting to the infinite imagination of the children to adapt each piece to a variety of games. The ever-popular tree house can be accessed by rope or ladder, challenging the physical skills of different age groups. A sand box and wood deck sits in the shade of the tree house for the enjoyment of the very smallest visitors to the playground. The sand also serves to pad possible falls from the tree house.

The play structures are constructed from durable materials such as white cypress pine, logs, natural stone and metal. All design includes detailing designed and assembled in accordance with Australian Standards.

Large Playground

Kaiser & Kühne

Heidepark, Soltau, Germany

photographs: contributed by HPC Ibérica S.A.

This large play space has been designed with children of all ages in mind, from three-year-olds up to even the young-at-heart adult. In order to meet this end the equipment had to have a wealth of content sufficient to attract both child and adult time and again.

The play structure is formed by a main tower measuring approximately 25 meters in height with five intermediate platforms set at heights of three, six, nine, twelve and fifteen meters.

Depending on the user's age, size and physical dexterity, there are various access routes – either via the spiral staircase leading from the base to each of the successive levels or by using one of the three large climbing nets, two of which reach the first platform at three meters' height, with the third leading directly to the second, six-meter level.

As far as getting down goes, the slide is always the easiest and most exciting option – here there are several to choose from. The smallest kids can use the two-meter-high wave slide at the bottom. Moving up to the third platform, there is a straight tube slide with rollers and polycarbonate windows or a curved tubular slide. From the fourth platform, users can zip down from a curved tubular slide with polycarbonate windows. Finally, two spiral slides drop fifteen meters down from the uppermost platform.

The long support beams in the main tower are in laminated timber, while the platforms feature horizontal laminated timber supports covered in locust tree wood. Hot strip galvanized steel and treated wood comprise the support posts for the slides. The stairs and vertical safety bars are stainless steel. The tubular slides are sheets of stainless steel of 2.5 mm width. The rollers on the slide leading from the third platform are 50 mm in diameter and have been mounted on interior stainless steel rails, creating a smooth tube that is entirely free from welded surfaces and edges. The stainless steel rollers do not require any further maintenance.

The climbing nets, with a web pattern of approximately 135mm X135 mm, are made from rope with a steel core. The support structure of the roof of the main tower is in steel. The decoration set atop the roof is in stainless steel with a stainless steel flag painted in polyester particles.

Central Park Playgrounds

Richard Dattner & Partners Architects PC

New York, USA

photographs: Richard Dattner

Among the first of a new generation of adventure playgrounds built in New York City, these play spaces allow children freedom of movement and physical challenges. A world in miniature — with mounds, streams, waterfalls, bridges and tunnels — these play settings let children exercise their imaginations and learn to master increasingly challenging environments.

Sand and water are essential components of these playgrounds — water providing movement, sound and color, and sand creating a safe play surface, which, when mixed with water, is a fun construction material.

Natural materials, simple forms and appropriately scaled spaces allow children to safely exercise their imaginations as well as their bodies.

The Central Park Playgrounds include The Adventure Playground at West 67th Street; The Ancient Play Garden at E. 85th Street; The Water Playground and Heckscher Playground at West 59th Street; The 72nd Street Playground on Fifth Avenue, and the Wild West Playground at West 91st Street.

Funabashi Wanpaku Park

PREC Institute Inc.

Funabashi City, Chiba Prefecture, Japan

photographs: Chiaki Yasukawa

Constructed to commemorate the 50th anniversary of the municipal government, the park is located in a particularly scenic landscape enjoying views of fields, a valley and abundant trees.
Two major themes dominated the planning process: providing appropriate stimuli for children's natural curiosity and development of the intellect on the one hand and, on the other, the idea that children should be encouraged to communicate with each other, as well as with nature.
The park's primary playing areas include the Castle play structure, the Water Study zone, which features Archimedes' spiral water pump and a pedaling water mill and, finally, the Small Animal Field, where children can visit a pasture and barn and go pony-back riding.

Plan

A. Sports Ground
B. Castle
C. Athletic Field
D. Water Study Facilities
E. Small Animal Field
F. Log Cabin Building Place
G. Nature Path
H. Tree-shade Field
I. Entrance Gate
J. Plaza

1. Fountain
2. Stream
3. Pond
4. Watch Tower
5. Gazebo
6. Pergola
7. Administration Office
8. Lavatory
9. Parking Lot
10. Suspension Bridge
11. Floating Bridge
12. Bank

Playground Pelzmühle Chemnitz

Rehwalat Landschaftsarchitekten

Chemnitz, Germany

photographs: Rehwaldt Landschaftsarchitekten

The new playground has been installed right in front of the entrance of the Chemnitz Zoo. The design aimed for a spacious rearrangement of the place, which confirms the importance of the zoo fort he city of Chemnitz.
The theme "Noah`s ark" is illustrated by five big animals and an abstract boat. The alignment of the figures in rows symbolises the walk of the animals into the ark.
The playground is partitioned into an equipment playing zone, a water playground and a zone for toddlers ("ark").
A curving bench marks the borderline towards the zoo entrance zone. It can be used for waiting for zoo visitors as well as for watching the children playing. Stylised animal figures are set up on prominent places to serve as direction signs along the way from the parking lot to the main entrance .

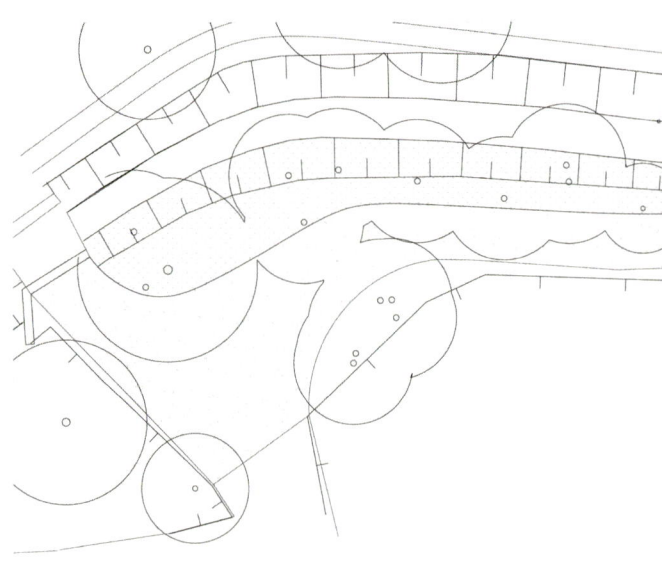

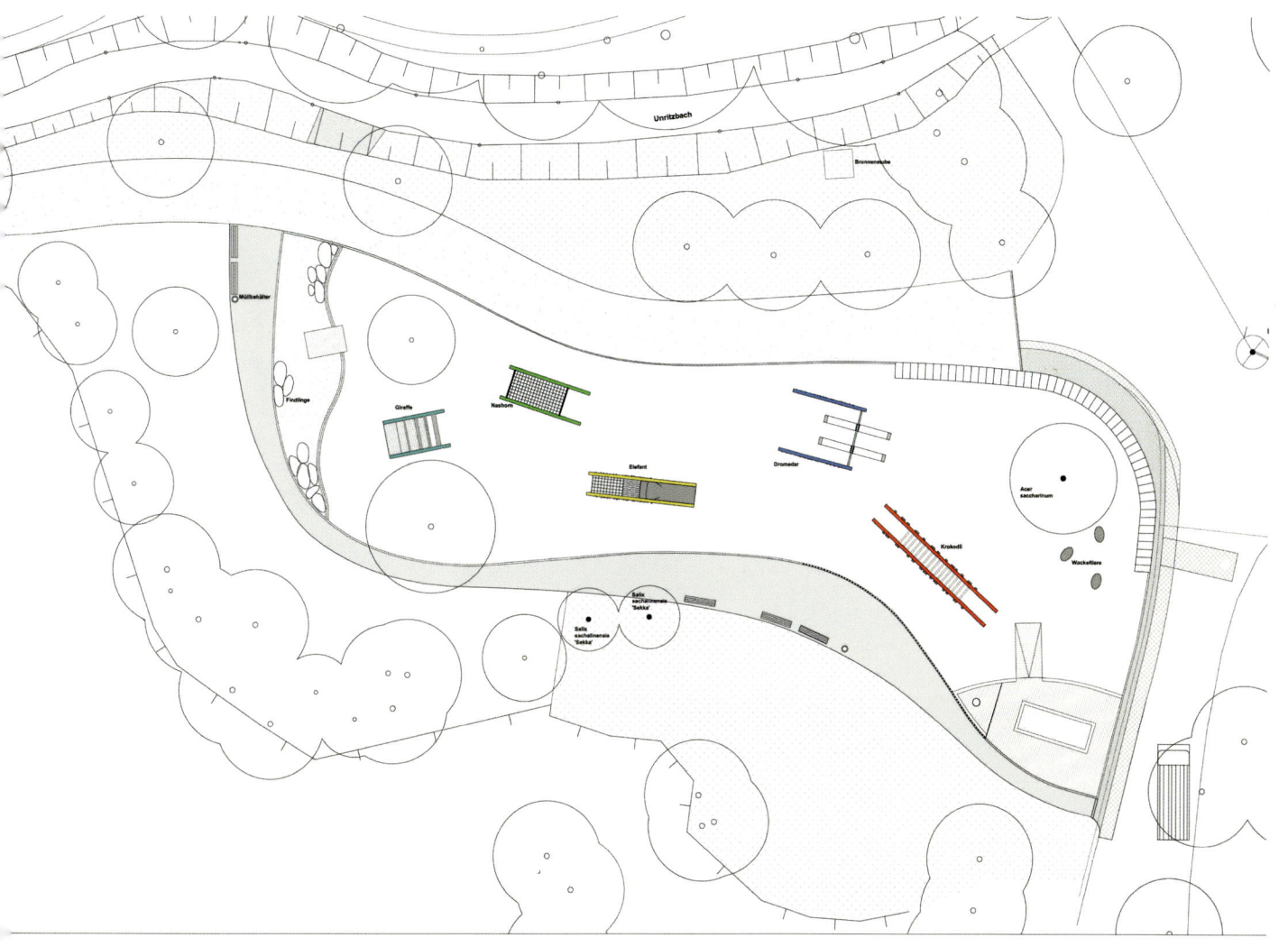

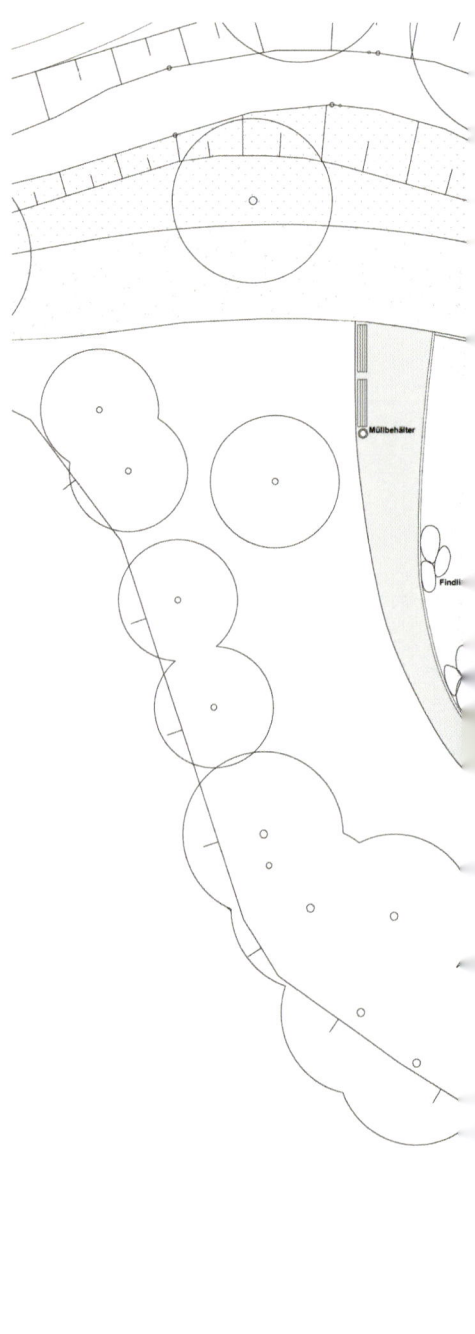

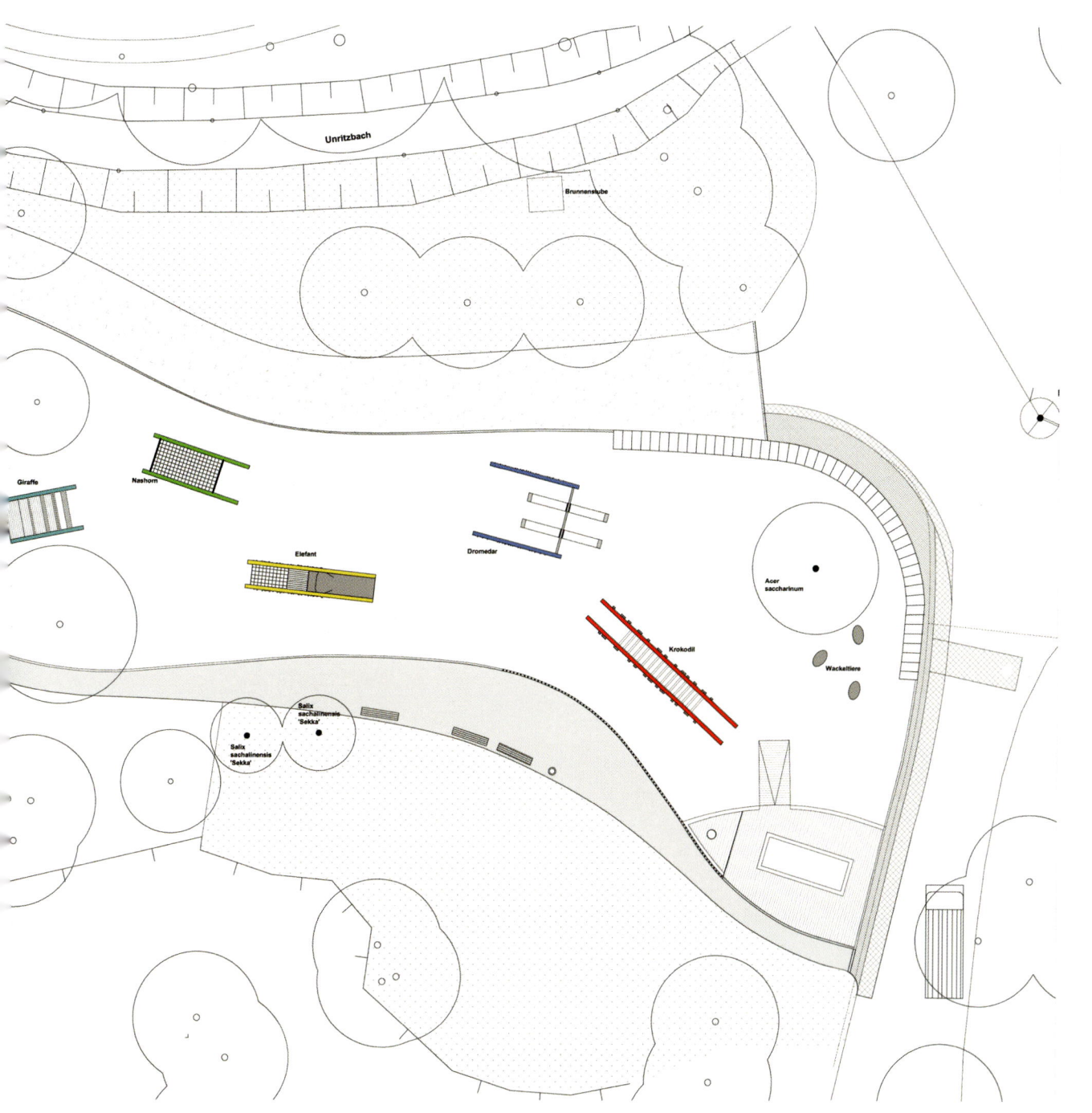

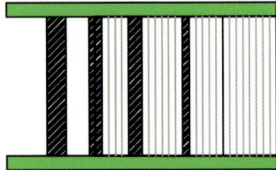
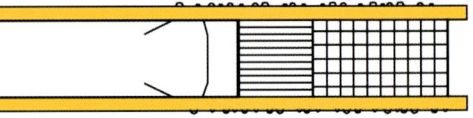
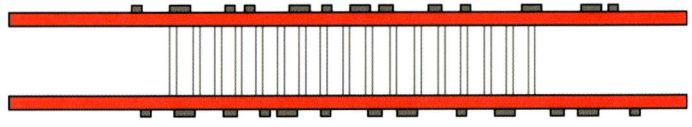

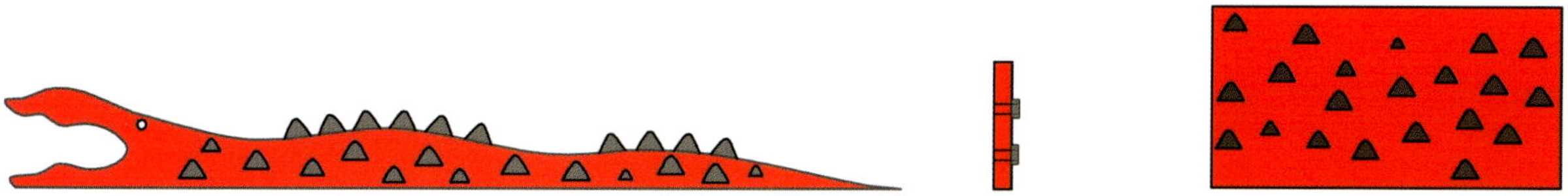

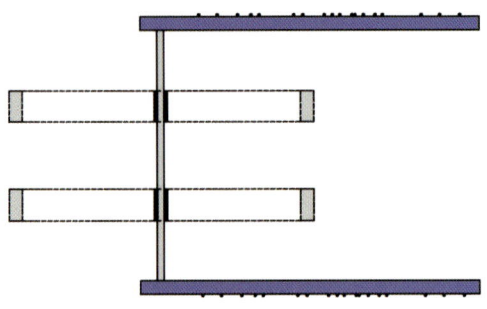

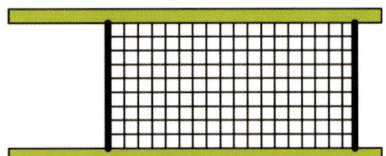

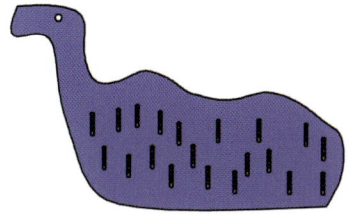

Go Green! - Environmental Play

architectureisfun, Inc.

Davie, Florida, USA

photographs:
Doug Snower

At Young At Art Children's Museum in Davie, Florida, children Go Green! From the start, the minute they press the traffic light to safely cross into the exhibit, children know this experience hits home. Go Green! Illuminates this avenue of learning. The familiar and reassuring house façade help instill the concepts of recycling in the home. The interactive learning stations demonstrate how to buy recycled products while teaching about curbside pick-ups for home recycling efforts. Children are prompted with questioning activities, which bring the presentation of the recycling process to a full circle. Children will make a game of learning how to repair, reduce, and reuse.

Ecology is really just a walk in the park in Go Green! In the Young At Art Park, children learn that you need to make responsible decisions about recycling when in public places. They will also learn how to use products made from recycled content. Reflecting upon the importance of doing your part, children perch on a recycled plastic lumber bench and then engage in responsible action. Indicating the correct environmental choice, children learn what can and cannot be recycled using the interactive, arcade buttons and signal panels. The trees in the park attract children; green and magnetic, they are the perfect place to be ecologically poetic, to express your feelings about protecting the environment and to draw upon the recycling-inspired vocabulary!

Kainan Wanpaku Park

Mitsuru Senda + Environment Design Institute

Kainan City, Wakayama, Japan

photographs: Environment Design Institute

Kainan Wanpaku Park is a sprawling playground set on a 91,000-square-meter site filled with numerous indoor and outdoor activities for children and adults alike. A massive spiraling path winds its way down from the hilltop toward the centerpiece of the complex: Kazenoko tower, encompassing 1047 square meters of total floor area distributed throughout two above-ground floors.

Located on the roof of the children's center, this tower play structure takes on a symbolic aspect while at the same time serving as a giant skylight that scoops natural light into the play center.

Built as a huge spiral, the tower's form echoes the spatial theme already established with the exterior footpath. Constructed primarily in steel, it comprises two major elements. One is the spiral ramp that allows a splendid view while climbing or descending; the other is the whimsical and varied interior with its nets, ropes, and other play items all set within the same spiral.

This project won the 2000 Wakayama Architecture and Landscape Award and the 2001 CLA Superior Award.

Kinder Museum / Zoom Ocean
ZEE

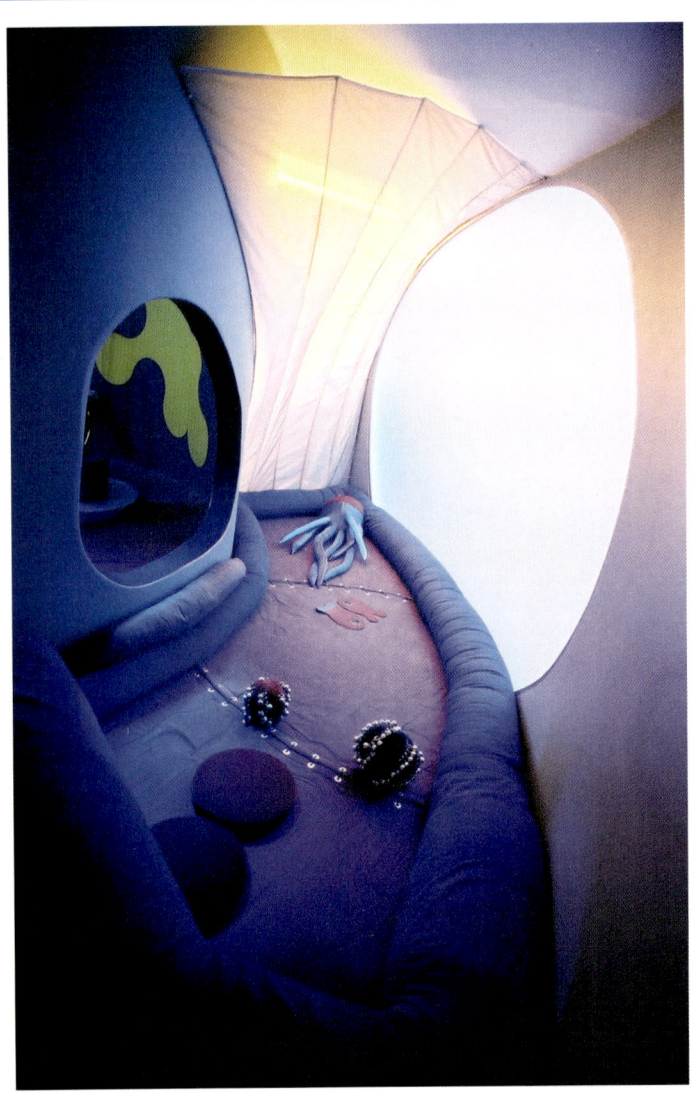

Wien, Austria

photographs: © ZOOM Children´s Museum

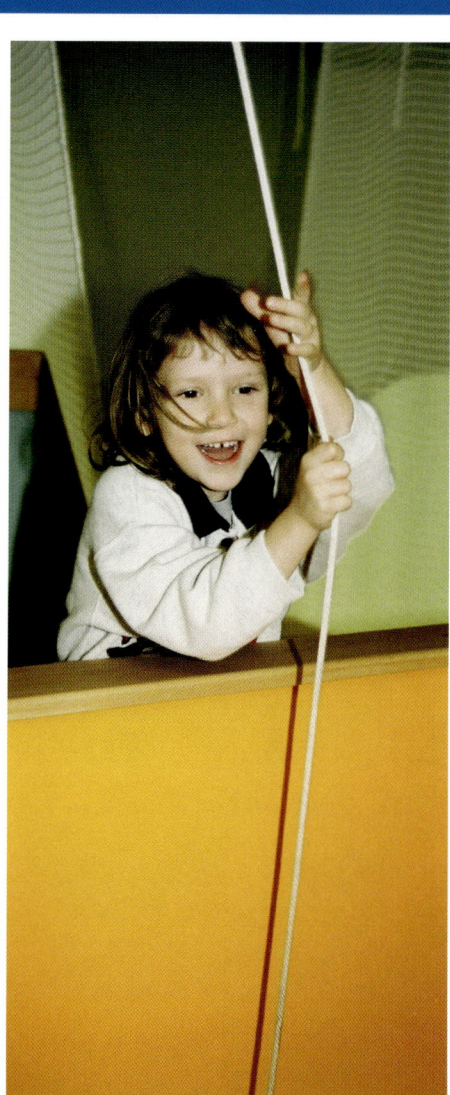

ZOOM Ocean, the Children's Museum's area for young children, invites young visitors from 0 to 6 to play, to explore and to dive into another world.
In the parallel world of ZOOM Ocean, young children have access to experiences that aren't possible in their (and our) usual environment. As they gather experience, ZOOM's youngest visitors conquer and slowly take over the different parts of ZOOM Ocean. From the underwater world onto the ship, from the ship to the reef and onto the island.
Baby Island is designed as an area for toddlers as well as a place of communication for parents and accompanying adults. Among beds of seaweed and sea anemones, toddlers learn to move their bodies on various surfaces and non-obstacles. They can refine their mo tor skills by practicing a wide range of movements. They jump and dive in the underwater world and playfully learn to handle space and perspectives.
Explorers discover and survey mysterious caves, grope their way in and out, and listen to the sounds of ZOOM Ocean. The children's sense of direction and physical coordination are practiced playing on tippy-toes with other divers. Further activities available on the coral reef foster haptic, spacial and cognitive-linguistic perception.
Out of the water and onto the ship! The kids take on roles and act them out in fantastic worlds, where they play along rules they make up themselves. They catch fish, throw anchors, steer the ship, learn how to deal with similarities and differences and feed their imaginations with real-life data - their own and those of others. It's up to the young sailors themselves if they want to navigate and manoeuvre the ship, establish radio contact with the Lighthouse or unload goods - and they have great fun even when they are shipwrecked.
At ZOOM Studio, kids find the motivation to develop ideas and to give full rein to their imagination. The atmosphere at ZOOM Studio is very special: No one tries to hold the children back; quite on the contrary, they are free to give shape to their dreams and ideas in their own terms.
ZOOM Studio is directed at preschoolers as well as 7-to-12-year-olds. Young artists and experts provide encouragement and motivation. Together, kids and artists playfully approach artistic concepts. And while all kinds of issues are explored, the important thing is to make the kids curious. All senses are involved in the process of creative production that follows.

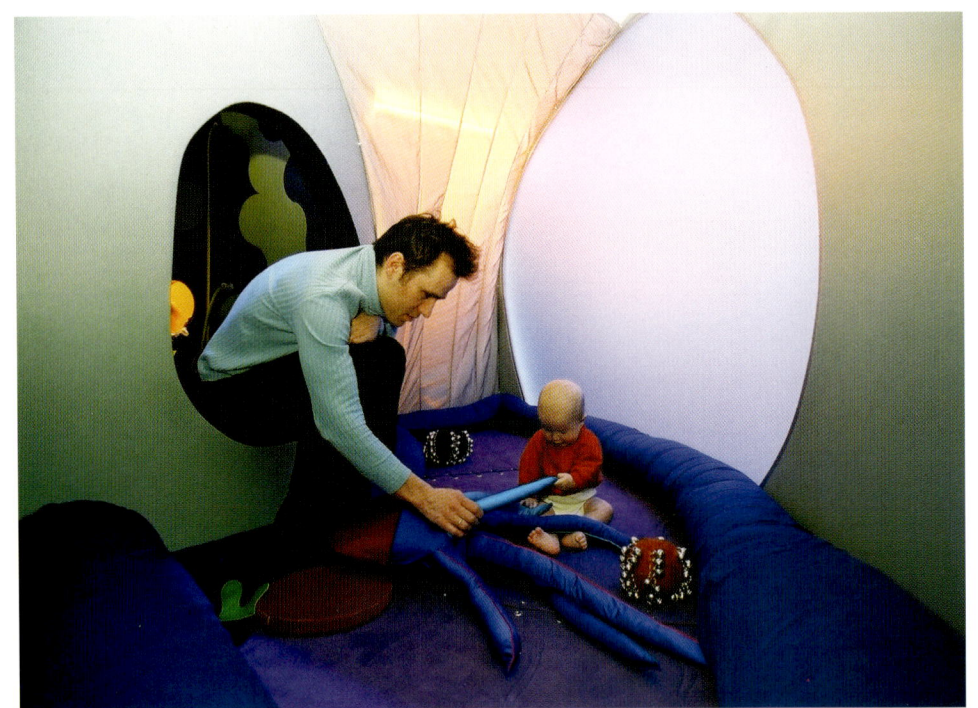

The Louisville Science Center Fit Project
architectureisfun, Inc.

Louisville, Kentucky, USA

photographs: Doug Snower Photography

Growing health and weight concerns led to the development of this traveling exhibit, which delivers the "Get Fit" message in fun and challenging ways. Geared for 8- to 14-year-olds, an age group that spends an average of four hours a day in front of TV's, computers, and video games, FIT gets hearts pounding and bodies moving. The "core box", a series of climb-on interactive activities, challenges notions of who is fit at work.

Are you as flexible as a dancer? Stretch. Do you have the heart and cardiovascular ability of a firefighter? Climb 60 steps a minute. Open the shipping crates, loaded with equipment from jump ropes to balance boards and test your abilities. Dance, dance, dance on the pulsating dance simulation machine. Whatever you try, FIT can be FUN!

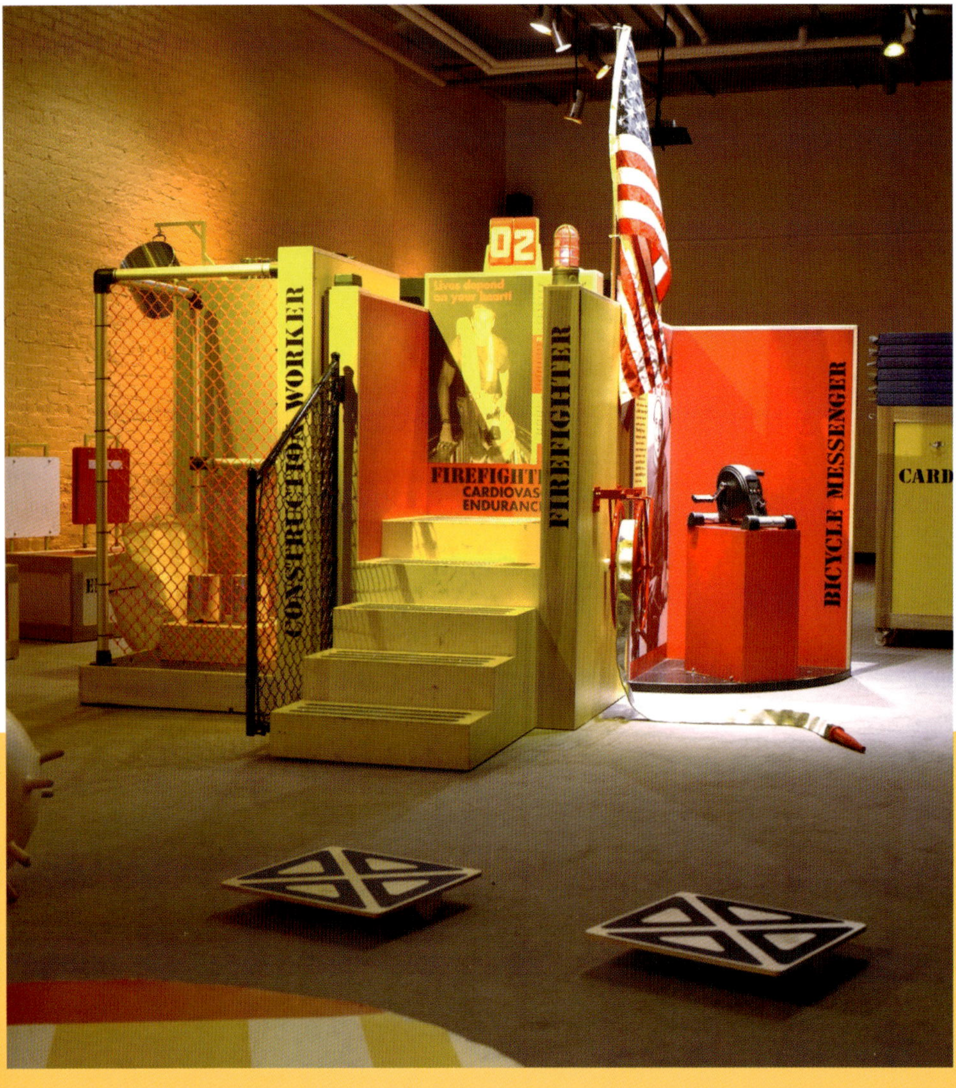
02
Lives depend on your heart!
CONSTRUCTION WORKER
FIREFIGHTER
BICYCLE MESSENGER

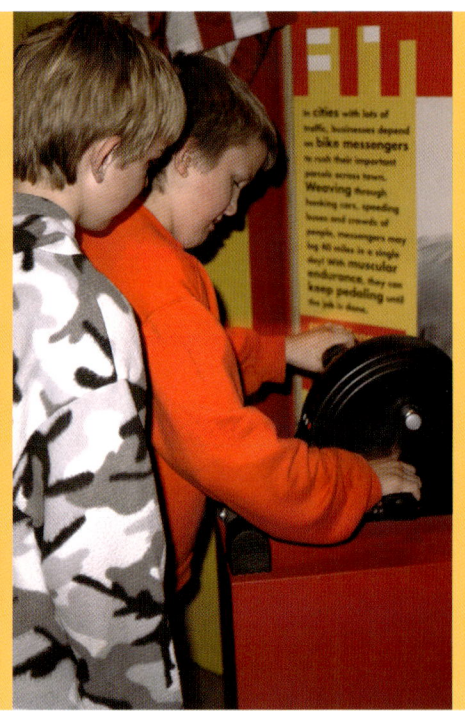

Toyama Children's Center
Mitsuru Senda + Environment Design Institute

Isui Town, Toyama Prefecture, Japan

photographs: Mitsumasa Fujitsuka

Located more or less centrally in a comprehensively planned park, this facility combines the kind of "hands-on" exhibition space found in children's museums in the United States with the kind of creative, activity-orientated children's facilities common in Japan.

Divided into three levels, the first comprises an activity space fostering creativity, the second a "hands-on" exhibition space, and the third a play space where there is a 100 meter long piece of play apparatus.

Aiming to create a space in which children of all ages would find their niche in which to play, it describes a figure eight on plan, with the roof of the building providing the chance to survey the surrounding area.

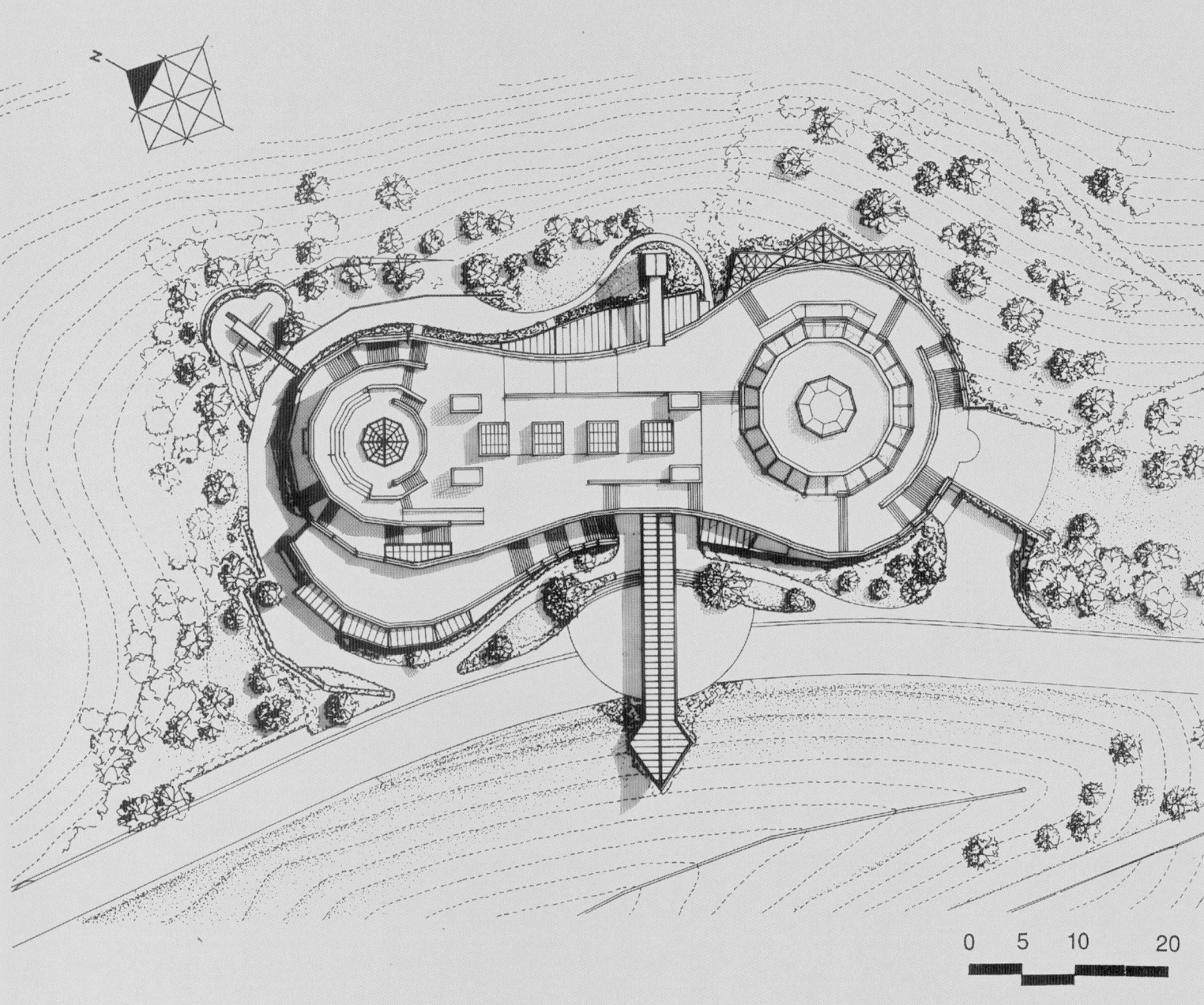

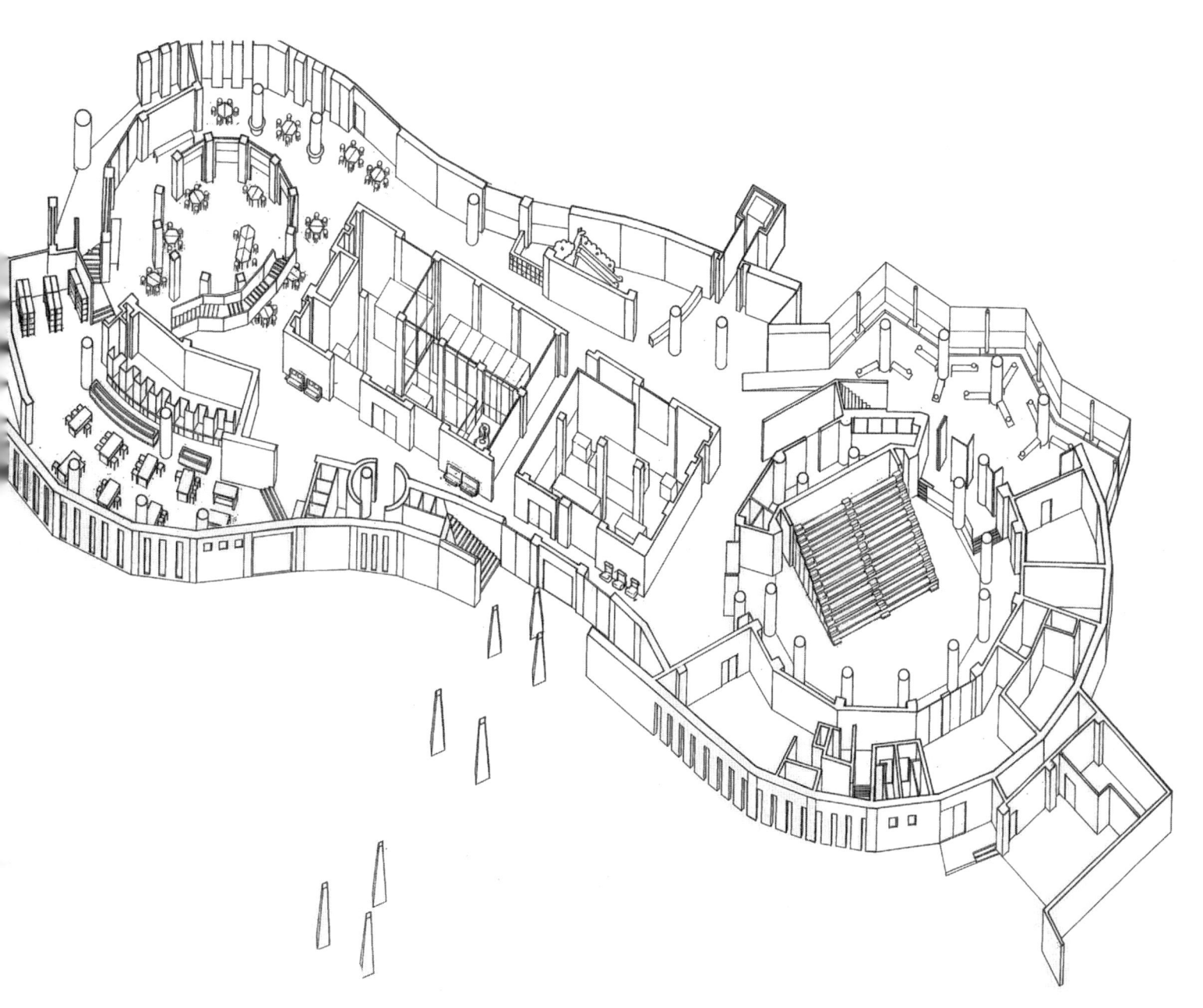

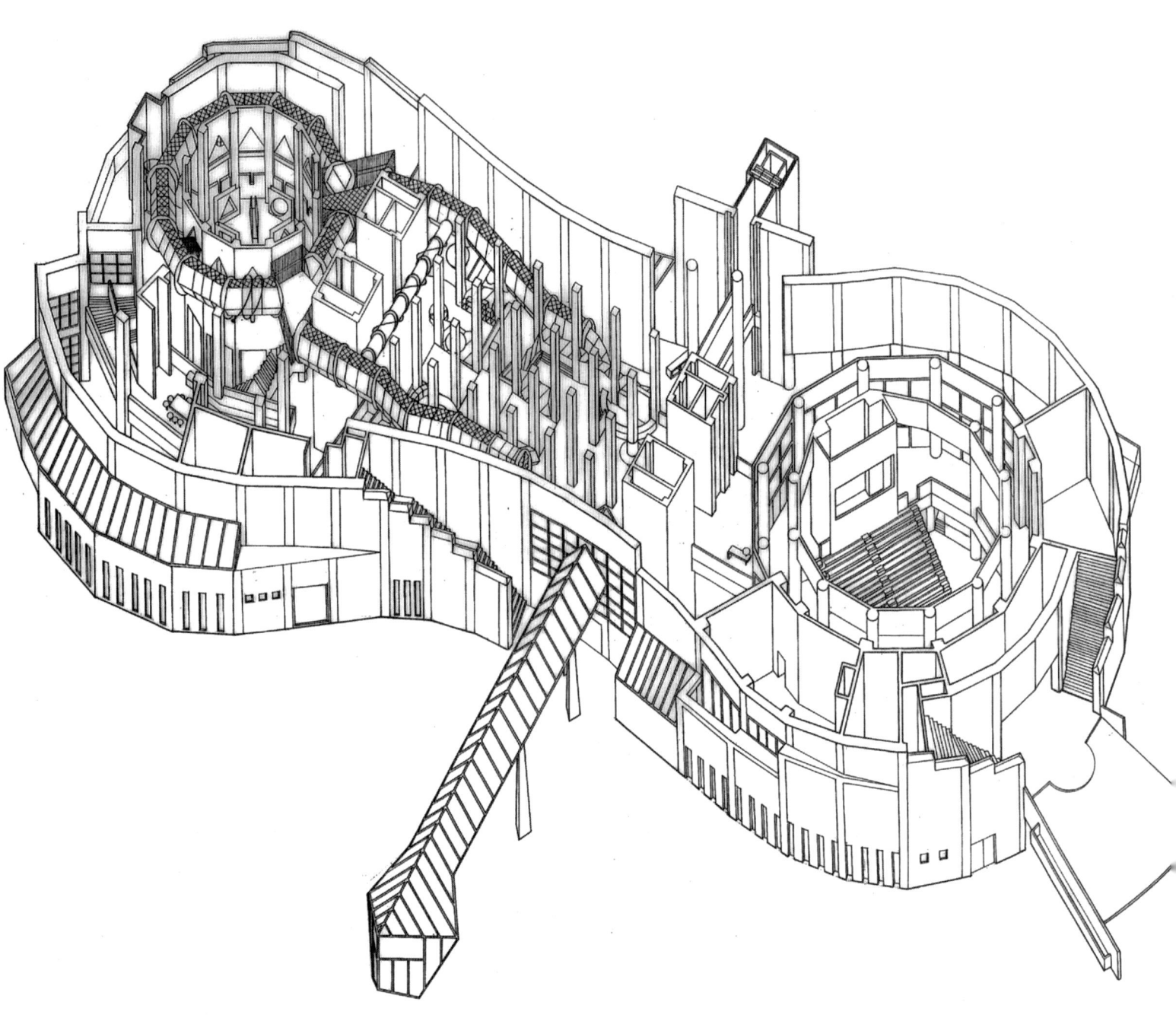

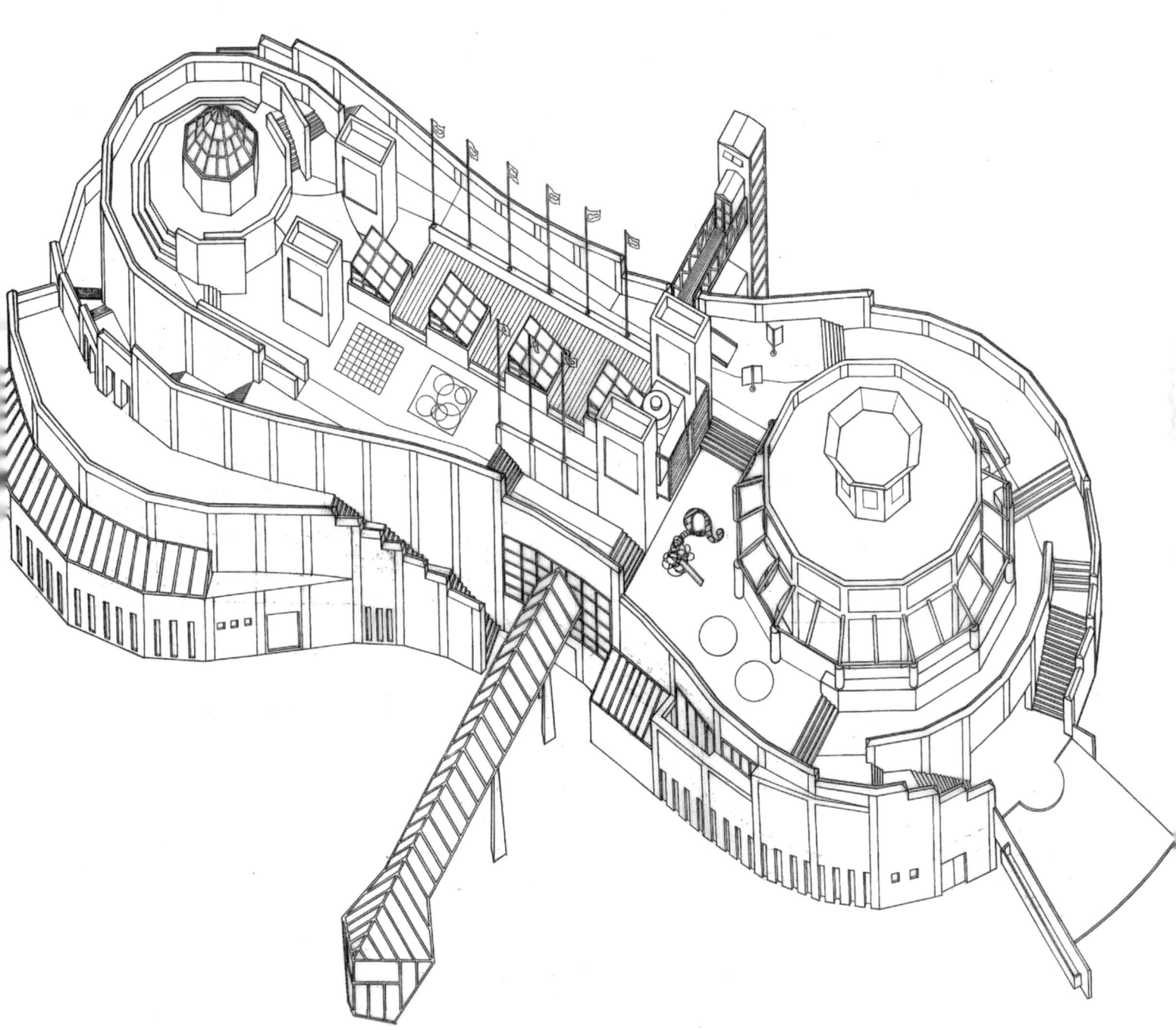

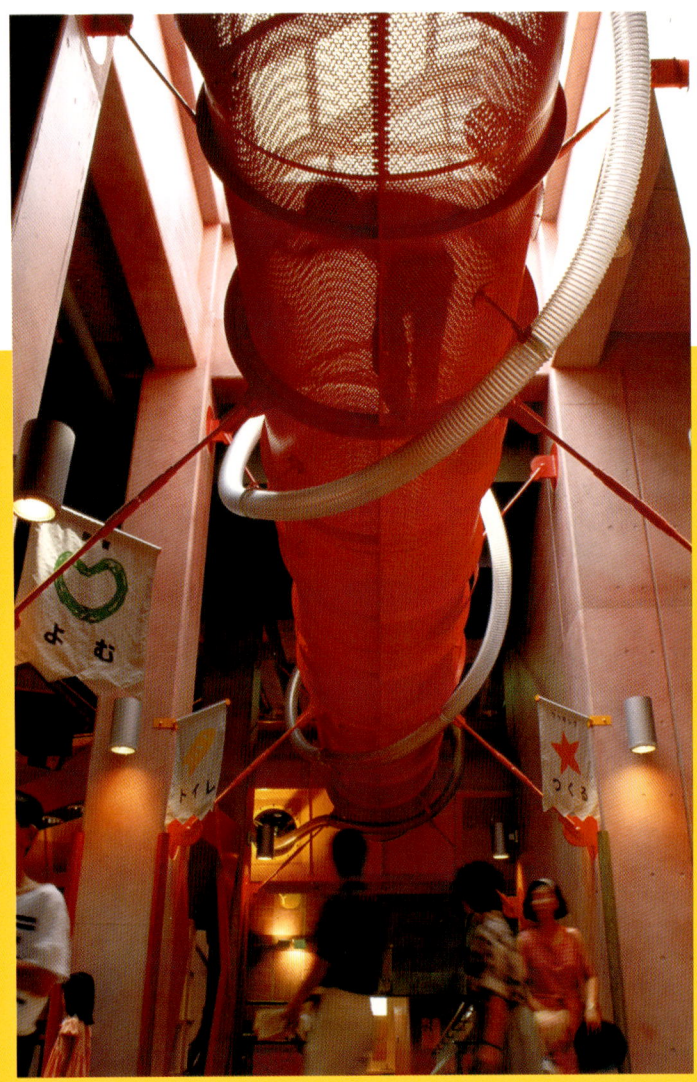

249

The Granger Community Church Children's Ministry

architectureisfun, Inc.

Granger, Indiana, USA

photographs: Doug Snower Photography

The new Children's Ministry Center at the Granger Community Church is mission-driven in both focus and design. The center promotes purposeful play, transmitted through design that uses biblical teaching as its foundation. Since opening, the children's attendance has increased over 60%.
Over 800 children fill the new center's 16,000 square feet of interactive themed environments, which have been grouped into five different categories that are age and purpose appropriate: the nursery where infants and toddlers focus on the high contrast trains and changeable landscape, 2-year-olds work the farm and harvest the crops, preschoolers wiggle through drainage pipes building with Noah's plans, kindergarten through second graders take off on an intergalactic mission and third through fifth graders become part of the church's Heir Force, performing and taking charge in a runway built for performance.

farm 1

farm 2

market 1

nursery 1

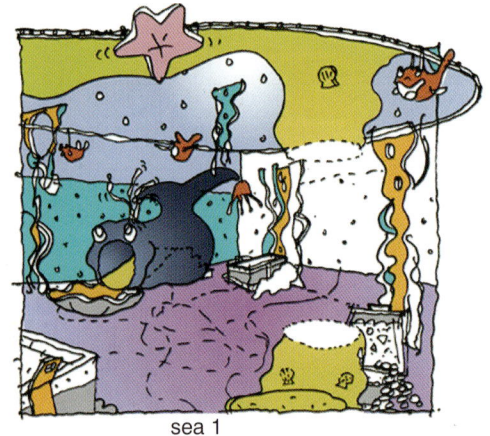
sea 1

sea 2

farm 3

nursery 2

virtuel

253

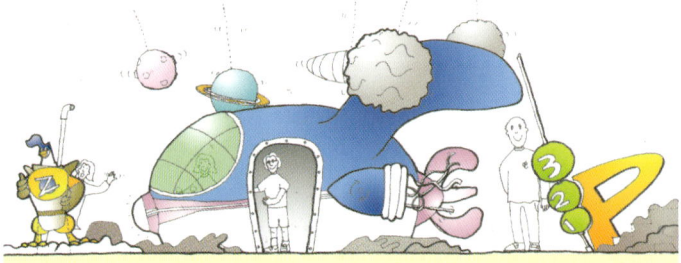

The Nursery Train That Could environment features tracks laid into the carpeting, taking toddlers through the space on train cars that have blowing smoke stacks, removable wheels, bells and whistles. The caboose plays lullabies and some cars are actually changing tables with mat, safety straps, diapering supplies and mobiles for capturing the baby's attention.

Floreix
Martirià Figueras

Girona, Spain

photographs: Martirià Figueras

"Temps de Flors" (Flower Time) is an annual event that fills the streets of Gerona with colorful temporary installations centered on a floral theme. For one week residents and visitors to the city can wander the streets of the historic district and enjoy the various stages set up by architects and designers. Not only are real flowers on display, but also the most unexpected objects are fashioned into plant-like replicas that are eye-catching in their own right.

Confronted with this parade of vibrant colors and natural fragrances, children are eager spectators that won't be satisfied with passive observation. The temptation is especially irresistible in this garden of giant flowers designed by Martirià Figueras. Children jump at the chance to participate in this enormous field of printed corollas, pretending to be bugs flying amidst the petals or jumping on them. Attuned to the laughter and comings and goings of the little ones in this fairy garden, many adults have to make an effort to stay on the sidelines. When the week of "Temps de Flors" is over, the installation is taken down in the real world, yet remains in the imaginations of the children.

Castle Park: temporary playground
Topotek 1

Wolfsburg, Germany **photographs: Hanns Joosten**

Castle Park was a temporary playground set up to entertain children while their parents visited the 2005 State Horticultural Show in Wolfsburg.

Twenty-four inflatable objects and fifteen cubes made of rubber foam colored pink and baby-pink are laid out on the lawn. Bogie wheels, rings, and air-filled wands, balls in various dimensions and two large mats with their exuberant color catch the attention and attract everyone willing to play onto the meadow next to a horse-paddock.

For the design-concept this close spatial proximity originally offered images of horse-books, girl romanticism and Barbie-world. The respective color concept was applied to the geometric forms. The inflatable objects are also flexible sculptures. The clear geometric forms contrast starkly with the fine textures of the leaves, grass and flowers. On closer approach the sensuality of the objects becomes tangible. They are soft, featherlike and seem harmless, tender even. The coated polyester fabric has a feel to it which can be conceptually related to the pink tones.

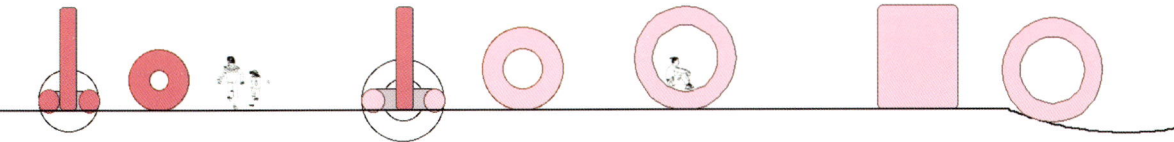

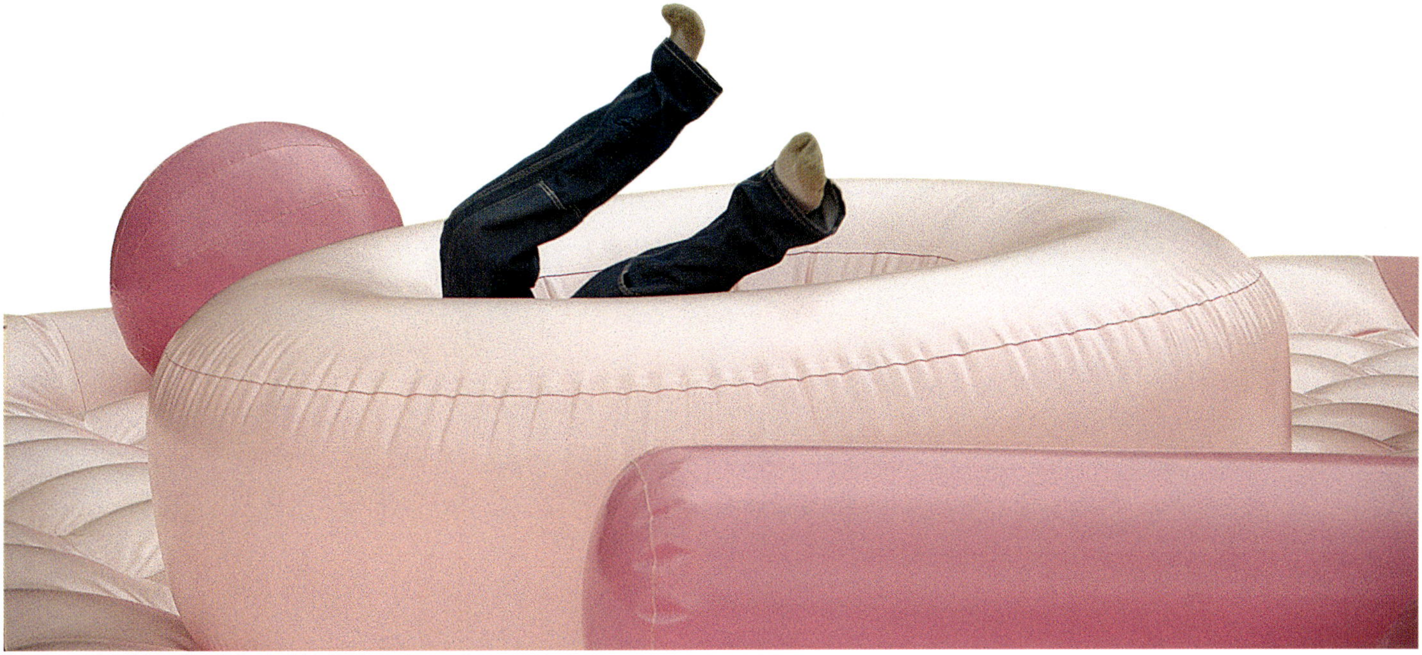

267